"Ebullient and enticing writing"

—Irina Moga, author of *Sea Glass Circe*

"A magical journey"

—Edythe Anstey Hanen, author of *Nine Birds Singing*

"A wholehearted delight!"

—Linda Quennec, author of *Fishing for Birds*

"An unforgettable journey"

—Annette LeBox, author of *Peace Is an Offering*

"Extremely well-documented with beautiful imagery"

—*Ottawa Review of Books*

"Definitely one of the best reads of the year"

—*CPR Magazine*

"Filled with adventure, history, and unforced hilarity"

—*New Reader Magazine*

"You won't want to travel with anyone else"

—Lorette C. Luzajic, *The Ekphrastic Review*

A SEASON ON VANCOUVER ISLAND

A SEASON ON VANCOUVER ISLAND

BILL ARNOTT

RMB

For information on purchasing bulk quantities of this book,
or to obtain media excerpts or invite the author to speak at an
event, please visit rmbooks.com and select the "Contact" tab.

RMB | Rocky Mountain Books Ltd.
rmbooks.com
@rmbooks
facebook.com/rmbooks

Cataloguing data available from Library and Archives Canada
ISBN 9781771605779 (paperback)
ISBN 9781771605786 (electronic)

Design: Lara Minja, Lime Design
Printed and bound in China

We acknowledge the financial support of the Government
of Canada through the Canada Book Fund and the Canada
Council for the Arts, and of the province of British Columbia
through the British Columbia Arts Council and the Book
Publishing Tax Credit.

For lovers of islands and coasts,
and all who live here.

VANCOUVER ISLAND AND BRITISH COLUMBIA GULF ISLANDS

Campbell River

Comox
Courtenay

Qualicum Beach
Parksville
Nanaimo
Port Alberni

Tofino

Ladysmith

Sidney

Shawnigan Lake

Victoria

CONTENTS

INTRODUCTION

First things first. This is a part of the world that I love. Vancouver Island and its surrounding archipelago, British Columbia's Gulf Islands, remain one of the planet's most magical regions. When RMB publisher Don Gorman asked if I'd write a memoir about time spent here and include original visual art, not only was I delighted but eager. Truth be told, I'd have created it anyway. Only now we can experience it together. Which is an incredible privilege, sharing vignettes and painting-style photos, discovering new and familiar sites: forest, sea, the lands of Indigenous Nations. I've included a note as to names and transliteration, doing my best to accurately relay regional narratives. The result, I feel, is a time-bending, present-day journey, imagery of place and people, recollection of the past while glimpsing the future. Meanwhile, the star of this show, the Island, in fact each island and coast, continues to reveal remarkable, intimate secrets. It's a sensory excursion I'm grateful and pleased to share. A season I hope you enjoy. ❧

TEN THOUSAND HORSES

A feeling of departure, and possibility.

Ten thousand horses rumble to life. With a diesel vibration, water churns into chop and a blue and white ferry shoves us into the strait, in the direction of Vancouver Island. On the other side of the water, Nanaimo. Snuneymuxw. Coast Salish land. A sense of connection is what I feel, gazing through open steel portals. The horses pick up their pace, trot to canter, as a ripple ricochets through rivets and railings. The result, a feeling of departure, and possibility.

It's what I felt as a child, venturing into hills behind our home on a north arm of Okanagan Lake, bubbles of land carved by glaciers, the big lake fed by a narrow, deep creek. It was that sense of departing on a grand adventure that's never gone away, each time I'm off somewhere new. Even places familiar, for that matter, seen for the first time again. As a kid I'd pick a stick from the deadwood, pry my way through barbed wire like a wrestler entering the ring and climb. Over the hill cattle grazed, and the land beyond that was orchard. It always smelled dry. Of course, I'd take care, watching for cow pies, rattlesnakes and undetonated mortars. An army camp was across the lake, and a few decades ago the arid grass banks served as target practice, bombs lobbed across the water.

Now, aboard a westbound ferry, the day's rolling out somewhat dreamily. The ferry is full, the first at capacity in months, and the crew's a bit overwhelmed by an onslaught of passengers awaiting their Triple O burgers, like kids released into summer following a particularly miserable winter. A winter that's lasted two years.

Our vehicle is on an upper deck berth aboard the MV *Queen of Cowichan*, and we've chosen to stay put, hunkering in our well-worn car, with the aroma of road trips, fast food and bare feet. Meanwhile, Horseshoe Bay's showing off its photogenic cliffs and arbutus, copper-pistachio peelings of bark as though they've been outdoors too long, overdue for a coating of sunscreen. Bowen Island rises from sun-dappled water like a child's likeness of a surfacing whale, a round hump of a back, the only things missing being flukes and a blowhole waterspout. Sounds and smells mingle, wafting amidst cars: cell phone chatter, sneaky second-hand smoke, laughter, coffee, the vibrating basso of ferry engine, and the inevitable bleat of a car alarm, its owner nowhere to be found.

Tatters of cloud stream past as we venture west by southwest. Midway across the Salish Sea we pass our doppelganger going the opposite way, the visual striking. A weather front's hanging in place at the halfway point of the crossing, a vertical line of rain and smudgy dark cloud, monochrome seascape in a rinse of blue-grey. I watch the ferry pass through the wall of weather, easing from dark to light, like Dorothy stepping from blustery Kansas to the Technicolor of Oz. Unbeknownst to me we're making our very own leap through a time-bending lens, as we've come for five weeks but will go home in three months from now. ❧

RAIN SPATTER
TO DELUGE

One milkshake is never enough.

Rain in light spatters greets us as we rattle down the ferry ramp, increasing to downpour as we make our way north and west from Departure Bay. It's late afternoon and we stop in Parksville for burgers, which we take to the beach, and a big wet log becomes seating and table in one. Remarkably, the rain stops for eight minutes, the exact amount of time required to consume a grilled burger from Dairy Queen. If you ever get a chance to try their butterscotch cones, don't. Unless you like the taste of iron and manganese, in which case, enjoy. The moment we're back in the vehicle, rain resumes, as though it paused just for us.

DQ was one of the first fast food restaurants in my hometown, and a favourite of Dad's and mine. We'd drink chocolate shakes and eat burgers with fries. Later, Dad learned from a friend to always order two milkshakes, as one's simply never enough.

This part of Vancouver Island is known for beaches and sandcastle building, the serious kind teams work on for days where there's actual money involved. Tourists come from afar to wander the maze of summertime structures, remarkable feats of beachside engineering and design. A far cry from childhood days when an upturned bucket would make for a turreted castle, a small stick or shell its flag.

The home I grew up in on Okanagan Lake was built by the water, a beachfront of weeping willows in amber, grass resembling lawn, and a shoreline of rock with a patch of coarse sand, the sand we used for castles. Beyond that, in the shallows, was a small but deep pit of mud in which you could wiggle your toes to make a wet squishy farting sound that made us laugh for years. ❧

RIO DE GRULLAS

A marriage of beach and towering pines.

The **Parksville area's been inhabited** for millennia, home to Coast Salish Nations including Snuneymuxw, Snaw-naw-as and Qualicum. The Spanish were here in the late eighteenth century, then George Vancouver arrived, planting British flags. Go far enough back in European records and you find Spanish names on sites of the Salish. One I like is Parksville's Englishman River, what we're crossing now, which had the Spanish name Rio de Grullas. River of Cranes. What the name givers saw were great blue herons that still ply the water, spear-fishing like darts in the shallows, their wide-winged flight the flap of pterodactyls.

Rathtrevor Beach Provincial Park hugs a convex curve of coast, a marriage of sandy beach and stands of towering pines. A few years back, my wife Deb and I bought a small trailer up the road and brought it here, to Rathtrevor. It felt like an easy way to get familiar with our new home-on-wheels a short distance from where we purchased it. We fell in love with the trees, skyscraping Douglas fir. It was spring, cold and damp, and the best I could do with wet wood was a fire of cleansing smoke, but it did keep mosquitoes away.

The beach is two kilometres long, enough to accompany a campground full of families, although at the time we had it to ourselves. Our little trailer, a wheeled micro-apartment, became our mobile residence for the next few summers. Topped with a solar panel and equipped with toilet and shower, it made us nearly self-sufficient, provided a grocery store was close by. Memories of food from those times are what linger: wild garlic scapes I gathered for pasta, and a fresh-caught trout we added to salad with blueberries, enjoyed with a water view. The trailer felt like five-star accommodation following a few seasons camping in the back of our vehicle, which was a smallish SUV. We jammed in a double-bed mattress that curled at the edges and felt like being swaddled, bedding down in a cushiony nest. We never slept better.

Now, still in Parksville, we're making our way up island. The Oceanside Route along here is a string of RV dealers, campgrounds, motels and fast food. There's a mini golf course with ubiquitous windmill, a giant shoe and water-hazard pools the colour of vibrant blue dye. This used to be John Hirst's land. He was the first European to claim property here, acreage straddling Englishman River, the river of crane-like herons. Hirst, like many white settlers in the area, was an industrialist, and made Nanaimo his home. The river was the throughway, along with the coast. A road wouldn't be here until the 1900s, linking it to Nanaimo. Logging drew new settlers with a railroad following, part of the E&N Railway, the Esquimalt-Nanaimo line. A post office was built, a fellow named Parks its first postmaster, after whom Parksville is named. The railway sparked the area's growth, but as in much of BC, resource industry shifted to tourism over the next century, and Parksville, with its pristine beaches, was destined to lead that transition. ❖

WHERE THE CHUM
SALMON RUN

A hummingbird that's somehow familiar.

Packing for this excursion was simple. Deb and I threw an armload of clothes in a duffle along with trail shoes and a stack of new books. Our accommodation for now is a small cottage in the woods of Qualicum Beach, a copse of cedars keeping company with spruce, fir and hemlock. The neighbours, we soon learn, are a family of warbling eagles, two owls who hoot hello, and a hummingbird that seems somehow familiar. There are songbirds as well: sparrows and chickadees, inverted wrens that nibble things from cedar strips, and a nondescript black and white bird with a monotone call and coquettish tail, the look of a folding fan.

Getting here, we'd stopped at a highway service station on Nanoose First Nation land, featuring a Snaw Naw As gift shop. We bought a mug with a red bear design, a creation of artist Jonathan Erickson of the Nak'azdli Band of the Gitksan Nation. An engraver and jewellery designer, Jon incorporates

Haida design in his work, one of his influences being Tsimshian artist Roy Henry Vickers.

A second mug we picked up is adorned in hummingbirds, Indigenous design by Ben Houstie of the Heiltsuk Nation, also known as Bella Bella or Waglisla. Ben is a painter and carver whose work reminds me of pieces I found on Haida Gwaii. It was the first time I'd seen Indigenous design featuring hummingbirds, symbolic of beauty and love. Referred to as Sah Sen, the tiny bird is a sign of friendship and play, a messenger of joy, hinting at what's to come.

As we crunch up a gravel drive through the corridor of trees, our temporary home resembles a fairy tale, and I keep an eye out for red-hooded girls and cross-dressing wolves. The little woodland abode has a fuchsia pink door, flowers in windowsill pots and a shiny red barbeque that must be brand new. This accommodation's a pendulum swing from camping when I was a kid. One of our favourite destinations was a cabin, high in the hills in south-central BC, Interior Salish land. We fished for deep water trout, which we smoked, and slept to the snap of mousetraps.

Here, from our pink-doored cottage, we can stroll to the seaside of Qualicum, what original inhabitants knew as the place where the chum salmon run. The shoreline stretches northwest and southeast in a wide, gentle curve. At low tide, morning sun glints on ribbons of kelp in pink, ivory and Celtic shades of green. Farther south is Parksville and beyond that, Nanaimo, where our ferry arrived from the mainland. A string of seaside communities lies to the north: Qualicum Bay, Fanny Bay, Union Bay and Royston. Beyond the inlet, islands sit like a hand of cards: Denman, Hornby and Lasqueti, with Texada adrift from the pack, as though discarded.

The tide moves a long way here, leaving a broad swath of beach. High tides offer good swimming, the water particularly warm now in the midst of record-breaking heat. Low tide reveals soft and walkable sand, the kind that demands you take shoes off and move slowly. Sun bakes exposed beach at low tide and then, as tide rises, heated sand warms the water. As a local explained, "It's a swimming pool, with a tide."

A steep set of stairs, about eight storeys' worth, connects a bend in the road to the beachside and makes for a good workout with ocean views. A tiny lending library, painted in rainbow colours, sits atop the stairs, where an abacus helps stair climbers keep track of their reps.

"I'm blue," a woman explains by the abacus, as she tackles the stairs. Which doesn't mean that she's glum but she's using the blue line of counter beads.

Today I'm yellow. Not sure why, but it feels fitting. Perhaps a sunny disposition.

Directly overhead, a bald eagle circles, casting a shadow with each pass while a crow makes a fuss, buzzing the big bird in flight. Following a few sets of stairs, I throw myself into the sea, and as I bob in the water a seal swims up and gives me the eye, but keeps a respectable distance, as though taking care not to spook me. ❧

SWIRL OF SARGASSO

A mesmeric whirl of green.

Nestled in our gingerbread home, I go online and order fish for curbside pickup nearby: local steelhead, sablefish, cod and some eel. I feel an obligation to add the eel as I'm reading Patrik Svensson's *The Book of Eels*. A few hours later I pick up the fish, including the packet of eel, a long, slender strip of plastic-sealed cardboard that, I decide, makes an excellent bookmark for my book about eels. Moments later, I've eaten my bookmark (it was delicious), forcing me to start the book once more from the beginning.

It's one of several I picked up at Qualicum's Mulberry Bush Book Store. Barb and Tom own the store and asked if I'd pop in to sign some books. I said I'd be happy to sign them all, but they insisted I only sign books that I've written.

One of the things I love about the store is you can access it not only from the street but also through a lush hedge of green, a pedestrian throughway that makes you feel you've happened upon a secret, someplace magical. I'd plucked *The Book of Eels* from the window display and at the till Tom and I traded one-liners.

"*Not* another book about *eels*?!"

"Yeah, need to make room on the shelf with all my *other* eel books!" And with a grin I took my new book to read on some grass by the sea.

Svensson weaves an engrossing narrative, part memoir, part zoological analysis of the mysterious eel, one of the most historically studied yet enigmatic creatures in the animal kingdom. Metaphors abound, but like the elusive, water-mottled protagonist of this non-fiction story, nothing is obvious. Only there, perhaps, if you care to see it. Through it all, a methodical and progressive revealing of experience and growth, not unlike the selective sexual maturation, fluidity and somewhat open-ended life cycle of an eel. From the philosophy and analytics of Aristotle and Freud to fishing weirs and the cutting-edge science of modern-day commerce, we find the eel ever present and timelessly evasive, its life beginning and ending, we believe, in a swirl of oceanic sargasso. Simply reading the words I find myself transported, the mesmeric whirl of green pulling me, tide-like, to fishing with Dad. The oar-lock squeaks that may well have triggered my personal viking pursuits, voyaging much of the planet, trailing a theoretical line like a sailcloth anchor at sea. ❖

VULTURES ON
THERMALS

Boulders overhead, colliding on ocean floor.

From **Qualicum I drive to Parksville,** sign some
more books, take photos and carry on south to
Nanaimo. Sun's radiant, windows are open and I've
got the radio blaring. Overhead, turkey vultures soar
fixed-wing on high thermals in languid pirouettes.
Having seen too many westerns, my first thought is
one of concern. *Vultures circling? Should I be worried?*

Last time I was here it was for spoken-word poetry
gigs and a multimedia show of live music and story-
telling. I'd arrived on foot, having gotten here by
float plane. The trip from Vancouver's Coal Harbour
to Nanaimo Harbour felt like a high-end amusement
park ride, a seat at the world's best fairground. That day
was like today, brilliant sunshine, a pleasant breeze.

With a daypack and a couple of books I'd ambled
my way, pre-gig, to a hostel. Later, after my perfor-
mance, I'd gone to an open mic stand-up comedy
night (to watch). The resto-lounge adjacent to the

hostel was doing its best to attract patrons on a weekday night. Like any amateur comedy night it was a mixed bag, some of the performers checking a box on their life to-do list, others serious about a career on stage. I laughed loudly, my way of being supportive. It also ensures I get left alone.

Until one of the comics pulled up a chair at the end of his set.

"Hey, thanks man. You really seemed to enjoy yourself!"

I congratulated him on doing what most people fear more than death.

"Right on. Thanks again, man!"

My only option then for a nighttime snack was the casino down by the waterfront. It wasn't particularly late, but fast food purveyors had already clicked over to drive-thru only. For a moment I considered it, but couldn't bring myself to be that middle-aged guy in jeans walking through the drive-thru. In fact, I don't think it's allowed. Funny, sure. But tragic.

So instead I made my way into the casino, through the epileptic neon flashes, *ka-chingle* of slots and lingering second-hand smoke, to the café, where I ordered a plate of salty things pulled from a fryer. The server was pleasant company, and as I was the only one there, I felt obliged to overtip, splitting the cash from my gig.

Now, back on the Inland Island Highway, the vultures have found new travellers to circle, and I take an exit to Nanaimo's town centre. Spain was again the first European nation to get here, exploring the area and renaming ancient locales, but leaving it to the British to resettle.

Two compact islands, Newcastle and Protection, sit just off Nanaimo's downtown. As the name of the first denotes, coal was the primary resource industry, drawing workers with much the same zeal as a gold rush. Seams of coal still run through the area, and an underground shaft connected Newcastle Island to the centre of town. Miners from the sea-submerged shaft would tell stories of hearing boulders collide overhead, tumbling on the ocean floor

Centring the old town is The Bastion, a squat wooden fort built in the 1850s. It's now dwarfed by apartments and a hotel but commands a good piece of land and remains a historic touchstone. Beyond that, Nanaimo's Waterfront Path, a seawall walkway, follows the shore for a pleasant five kilometres. From here, in the sun, Gabriola Island gleams in the southeast, its sheer bank of sandstone beneath Stony Ridge an ongoing point of contention amongst builders and environmentalists.

From The Bastion, I march up the hill to visit with Andrée, owner of Windowseat Books. As I arrive I feel I'm walking onto a movie set, one of those films where locals convene at a neighbourhood barbershop. Two folding chairs have been pulled out front of the store in the shade of a leafy maple, and the storeowner's chatting with customers and passersby, enjoying the space on this warm sunny day. A man's choosing a book for his granddaughter, something he does every few weeks, while a woman is checking on her special order. Another customer's pushing his baby in a stroller and asks if I'll sign his new copy of my book. Then we chat about writing, as he's currently completing the manuscript of his personal story of recovery.

I pick up Robin Wall Kimmerer's *Braiding Sweetgrass* and immerse myself in her poetic prose. Passages feel like a hike through forest, field and marsh, and I find myself wanting to plant things, no doubt what the author would love us to do. The text's not only consistent with the pace of much of this area but in keeping with the very nature of my exploration, peeling back a layer or two of these islands, tapping into the energy of people and place. ❧

A LATE VISITOR

Making her way, elsewhere.

Back on the road, I'm recollecting time spent in and around Nanaimo. One of our previous visits was a longer-term stay. Deb and I were here for a few months, late spring through early fall, but we pretty much stayed in one spot. It was another cottage in trees by the water, with one other home nearby. A narrow dirt trail bisected the lots and offered up shoreline access.

The accommodation was a small, stand-alone house with a glassed-in sitting room that felt like a greenhouse. The property was a short distance from Departure Bay, ferries coming and going to and from the mainland. As we dozed off at night, the rumble of the day's last ferry would vibrate the house, up through our mattress, like coin-operated beds in an hourly motel.

One night in particular, sleep wouldn't come. Aware of my fidgeting, I went to the glass-walled living room where I wouldn't disturb Deb. Eventually, I fell asleep on the sofa, surrounded amidst windows and trees, only to be woken by a dream. A dream in which an elderly woman glided into the room and stared down at me from above. Her face came close to mine and her look was one of curiosity, not frightening, just a little unsettling, and I woke with my hackles up high.

"Huh," was all I could muster. And went back to sleep.

Then it happened again. The woman gliding in, staring me in the face, with a calm but inquisitive look. Again I awoke, shook my head, muttered another "Huh," and dozed off once more. The third time it happened, I didn't go back to sleep.

"Right!" I said, and wished the woman peace. Then I marched back to bed, where I lay awake for the rest of the night, squished a bit closer to Deb, who was still sound asleep.

Two days later, I was out in the yard when a repairman arrived to work on the neighbour's power-line box.

"Everything okay?" I asked, as we'd had recent outages.

"Yeah," he said. "Just turning things off next door. The lady that lived here passed away two nights ago."

"Oh," I said, fairly certain that's who I'd met, hovering in our living room, as she made her way elsewhere. ❧

FOREST ART

———

The hummingbird, watching, wondering
when I'll be home.

Yet another blisteringly hot day. Today's forecast
is a high of 40 degrees Celsius. A headline in
the *Parksville Qualicum Beach News* reads, "Sidewalk
buckles in sizzling heat." There's a picture of the
space we walked the previous day, now snapped into
a high asphalt peak. I leave Deb in the relative cool
of the cottage, the cedars dropping the temperature
by ten degrees, and I wander the trails of Qualicum's
Heritage Forest.

Eagles chirp from a hemlock that seems to touch
a fine wisp of cloud overhead, while a woodpecker
hammers away at something with a *rat-tat-tat-tat-
tat*. A flash of colour catches my eye at the base of
a tree. Someone's done an art drop, small painted
rocks distributed along the trail. This one looks like
a beetle in rainbow stripes. Another resembles a butterfly, a flat stone painted gold and blue. Meanwhile,
the trees themselves could be an art installation.
There's a tall trunk, symmetrically split in two by

the elements like a massive wood flower opening in bloom. And a fir that grew up for a spell, then to the right for a while before changing its mind once again to continue straight up to the sky. Now it resembles a bicep, flexed in a perfect right angle.

From the forest I emerge onto a quiet road, tall trees on either side creating a visual vanishing point. And framed in the greenery, centred above the road, a hummingbird floats at eye level, watching, as though wondering when I'll be home.

Back at the cottage, the colossal cedars exude calming energy and I feel I'm on oxygen, breathing enriched new air. I admire an arborist's work, limbs sheared high up the trunk to let in light, and the surrounding ground cover is thriving. It reminds me of a Surrey townhouse we lived in, and our strata had called in a guy to bring down a tree, a tall, solitary cedar that was considered a risk of falling. I watched through a window as he climbed the tree, equipped in spikes and a logger's belt from which two chainsaws hung like huge keys. One of the saws he used for precision work, trimming branches like a barber tidying sideburns. And with the larger saw he hacked off the top of the tree, which fell like a dart to the ground, creating a sky-high flat stump. Then the guy, with chainsaws hanging from his belt, took a seat atop the stump, the blunt tree bending back and forth like a reed, and had his break, lingering over a cigarette and making a call on his cell phone, his wavering chair 15 metres off the ground. ❧

CHAMPAGNE
AND TRUFFLES

―――――

Jazz drifts from a small marquee.

Another wooded trail leads from our cottage into town, part of a shared footpath linking Qualicum to Parksville, allowing for a shaded stroll into the village centre. Which today is the site of a street sale, merchants with goods on tables along the main drag, spilling onto side streets and a couple of alleys. A young, skilled quartet play jazz from under a small marquee. As we join a flow of browsers and buyers, a smiling woman asks if we'd like complimentary champagne and truffle popcorn.

"Hell, yes!" I say, to which she laughs, pours me a glass and hands me a serving of popcorn.

When we had summertime sales on Main Street when I was a kid, I can assure you we never had champagne or truffle popcorn. As I munch and slurp I decide progress is a very good thing.

Some time later, Deb and I drive to the airport. No, we're not yet in transit. We've come for the restaurant here, a combination of indoor and out-door space, overlooking the quiet little regional airstrip. We chat with the server, marvelling at this gem of an establishment.

"Yeah," she says. "People fly in just for a meal. Small, single-engine planes. We had people in from Campbell River earlier. And others from Victoria, here for brunch. Then they fly home." ❧

A GLIMPSE
OF LANDS END

———

How many more, scattered around the globe?

A **cloudy morning,** the first we've had since leaving the mainland last month. Tomorrow will be a travel day as we make our way from Qualicum to the Saanich Peninsula, to a place on a road called Lands End. I've visited a few places now that share that romantic name, each invitingly unique, each uniquely inviting. And I wonder how many others there are, on shorelines and cliffs, scattered around the globe?

Despite this trip still being in its early stages, I feel a bit sad moving on, a touch of nostalgia in the present. The time we've spent in and around Qualicum has been exceptional. Perhaps because it started our tour of islands. Maybe it's the people we've met. Or the weather, ocean swimming in heat, then finding shade in the trees. Or that welcoming hummingbird. Each facet of the area, forest and sea, seems to nurture, replenish and rejuvenate. I'm surprised at how an upcoming two-hour drive now strikes me as an insufferable amount of travel time. How quickly we settle into locales, establishing new parameters. ❧

Sunrise Through Driftwood, Qualicum Beach

Inuksuit, Parksville Beach

Sunrise Through Smoke, Qualicum Beach

Barred Owl in Old Growth Cedar, Qualicum

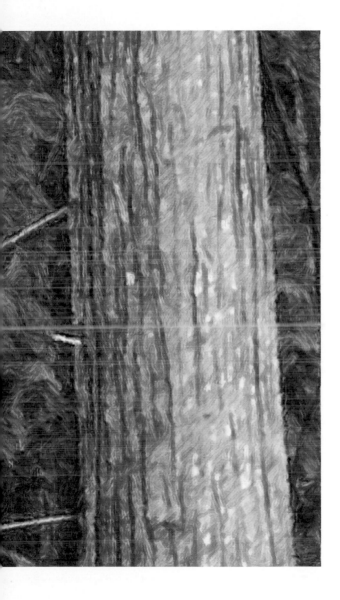

Qualicum Heritage Forest

PARALLEL FORTY-NINE

Our pace, no more than a shuffle.

We're heading south on Vancouver Island, or Big Island, before curving east and then north, our pace today no more than a shuffle. With a sightseer's mindset, I intend to stop at each viewpoint, eat ice cream and take photos of just about anything. We've driven partway from Qualicum and now, exiting the highway (which isn't much of a di version here), we drive into Ladysmith, Stz'uminus land. A town of hanging planters and shop fronts that resemble facades from the turn of the twentieth century. We're on the forty-ninth parallel here, and if we made a beeline due east across the Strait of Georgia, we'd land on the border separating BC and Washington state.

The town was originally called Oyster Harbour, and that name still appears on some signs. It's another region of forestry, agriculture and tourism, and while I can't contribute much to forestry or agricultural activity, I certainly know how to be a tourist. Heading up a low hill in the car, we enjoy a harbour view across the highway. The local bakery was recommended, so we join a queue and load up on baked goods: meat pie, samosa, pasty, quiche, salad and a couple of cinnamon buns. And no, this isn't our lunch. It's a bit of a stock-up for our next accommodation.

Strolling around town, we notice colonial history's prevalent. The present-day town was founded in the late nineteenth century by coal baron James Dunsmuir, owner of the mines around Nanaimo. He established Ladysmith to house his workers and their families, with access to mines by rail and water. Some of the buildings were prefabricated and brought here by oxen, others by locomotive.

The name Ladysmith comes from Britain's South African Governor Harry Smith's spouse, the wonderfully named Juana María de los Dolores de León, who took her husband's surname. And although this pretty seaside town could be named Juana María de los Dolores de León by the Sea, it's instead called Ladysmith. No doubt saving the city some money on signage.

In keeping with Dunsmuir's nod to the Boer War campaign, streets are named after British military personnel: Roberts, Buller, Kitchener, French, Baden-Powell and so on, generals and field marshals one and all. Despite a military history behind the monikers, the town now strikes me as resoundingly peaceful. But as in most places founded on industry, violence and unrest eventually arrived, consuming the area during a coal miners' strike that rocked Vancouver Island from 1912 to 1914. ❖

MEETING OF TRADITION
AND PEOPLE

Cars tethered with kayaks and trailers.

Our drive takes us farther south, a bit east and then north, our destination for now the Saanich Peninsula, Big Island's southeast spur. We could take a ferry across Saanich Inlet from Mill Bay to Brentwood Bay, but a quick Google search indicates it's the same amount of time for us to go via water or land. So today we'll stay on the road, where vehicles have a decidedly summertime look: vans with bikes on the back, cars tethered with kayaks, trucks with campers and trailers, and rig-sized mobile homes.

It's another hot day, and we're alternating between open air blasting through windows and spurts of air conditioning. Radio stations come and go, from North Island country hits to Nanaimo alternatives, occasionally signals from the mainland, and eventually Victoria radio dominates the dial as we follow the highway toward our provincial capital.

Despite the bakery stop, it's now time for lunch, and we've been looking forward to it for a while.

Songhees Food Truck ("Where People and Tradition Come to Meet"). A state of the art Songhees Nation event centre is located nearby on Lekwungen land, catering to groups, weddings and conferences. But today we're simply hitting the food truck, now parked on Songhees land on the snaggletooth west Victoria peninsula known as Esquimalt. The formula's simple, though few do it so well: a modern take on traditional cuisine, prepared with fresh, sustainable ingredients, served by a friendly, knowledgeable team of locals. Without exaggeration, the salmon burger changed my life. A beautiful fillet of sockeye, grilled perfectly, served with Saskatoon berry BBQ sauce, onion marmalade and stinging nettle mayo. Served on fresh baked Songhees bannock.

Deb and I take seats at a shared picnic table in the sun, exchanging friendly nods with other midday diners. There's not a lot of talk. People are here for the food. The energy is warm and welcoming, one of sharing. And with our first bites Deb and I simply chuckle, as this is some of the very best food we've eaten.

Driving leisurely into Victoria, we take time to suss out the area. The European-settled city, dating back to the 1840s, is one of the oldest in the Pacific Northwest. We navigate one-way streets through downtown and dawdle along in light traffic past the landmark Parliament Buildings and Legislative Assembly, the sea ever present, peeking around buildings and trees. Between boat traffic, float planes, tour providers and ferries, the harbour is one of North America's busiest.

This too is Coast Salish land, extending along the south and east of Big Island. Cruising through Chinatown, I learn it's the second oldest on the continent after San Francisco's. Our drive meanders us by the finger of harbour where Perez, Cook and Vancouver moored their fleets, and the Royal BC Museum, a pivotal point on my *Gone Viking* expeditions when I gawked at a travelling exhibit of long ships, treasure and artifacts brought here from Sweden. A map of the globe unfurled in my mind, spread on a mead-stained table, with imagined striped sails bent in the wind and the watery *whoosh* of ocean on steerboard, cutting its way toward Greenland.

We drive through James Bay and Oak Bay, past Beacon Hill Park, and putter the length of Cook Street, where a village vibe rules, storefronts eclectic and new, the gentrified feel of transition and comfortable wealth. The city's considered one of the best in the world for quality of life, but as in every city there's homelessness, and here as much or more than anywhere. It's also known as the Garden City, and driving through towering deciduous I can see why. Greenery meets overhead, creating leafy tunnels on side streets. We park at a pullout with a view of Discovery Island and the Oak Bay Islands Ecological Reserve, Haro Strait bathing the islands. Beyond that, an imaginary border on water separates countries on maps.

A walker goes past, slowly, singing at a maniacal volume, commanding space as she goes. We roll up windows and drive on, once more joining the highway. Only now we're going due north on the Saanich Peninsula, where we'll spend the next week and a half outside Sidney, in a basement suite with a water view, if the photos online are accurate. Proximity to Sidney is good, with its shops and restaurants, bookstores and seaside. After the past few weeks in the silence of forest (not counting the chatter of eagles and owls), the bustle and sprawl of city with an imminent buzz of ferry traffic feels harshly frenetic. And I find a citified state of mind encroaching, one I'd rather liked being rid of. ❧

SUN SETS ON LANDS END

---

*Whizzing and whirring, an explosion
of dance and sound.*

Turns out the photos online were accurate. Our new accommodation, the basement of somebody's house, looks through trees to the water, where ferries ease past from Swartz Bay. A blacktail doe and her fawn block my view, mind you, so I take a picture that looks photoshopped, almost too perfect. Another owl hoots from nearby, and a straggly tree at the edge of the yard is home to a busy hummingbird. (*The* hummingbird?) It flies up with a loud *whirr* and soft *cheep*, checks me out, then goes back to whatever it's working on.

As sun starts to set, we walk from our basement suite along Lands End Road, over the highway past Swartz Bay ferry terminal (with sailings to the mainland and Southern Gulf Islands), through a couple of traffic lights and down a curving road to a marina and restaurant patio. We haven't dined out for a while and we indulge: starters, cocktails, wine and big entrees. The food is fine, the service unre-markable, the cost substantial. Feeling as though we've done our part to support the local economy, we waddle our way home in the gloaming.

The light now is the same as when Deb and I stayed in a house in Peachland – another view of Okanagan Lake, but distinct from my childhood home. You see it, and smell it, travelling south through BC's interior, a transition from semi-arid to desert, a feeling of dryness and sand. That night we sat on a patio, sun setting behind us, tinting the lake in colours of orchards nearby, peach and plum and cherry. And as sky turned to black, a dozen hum-mingbirds flew around us, a tiny air show of *whizzing* and *whirring*, ups and downs at impossible speeds, a *Fantasia* explosion of dance and sound.

Next day I pop into Victoria to visit the team at Munro's Books, take pics and sign books (that I've written) then link up with Don, publisher at RMB | Rocky Mountain Books, to soak up some sun along Cook Street. Over a beer we chat about all the things people chat about over beer: Norse Sagas and Icelandic literature, the usual stuff. And of course fly-fishing. ❖

VANISHING TROLLS

Flowery lichen hangs from the trees,
our footsteps dampened by moss.

It's the weekend. Much of the world's watching the Euro Championship, but today's warm and sunny and a hill beckons from across the road. I set the TV to record the game, and armed with water and extra sunscreen, we climb our way into the trees of Horth Hill Regional Park, which becomes a favourite destination. Easy access, quiet, undulating trail patched in sun and plenty of shade. A loop trail circles most of the park with views of BC's Gulf Islands, America's San Juan Islands to the east, and the gentle blue chop of the Satellite Channel, flowing between the Saanich Peninsula and the double-hourglass shores of Salt Spring Island to the north.

Climbing the hundred-plus metres toward Horth Hill summit, named for one of the first European families here in North Saanich, becomes a pleasant sensory assault: the dangly pine, car-freshener scent of red cedar and fir, with leafy applause in the breeze from a canopy of Garry oak. The trail winds behind homes, never too far from civilization, but is sufficiently enveloped in swordfern and maple to create a feeling of remoteness and privacy. Butterflies keep us company, along with noisy robins tossing through leaves in thickets. Lichen hangs from the trees while our footsteps are dampened by moss and loose dirt on the trail.

Another couple, a woman and man, are on the path, walking in our direction.

"Have you seen the fairy tale?" he calls ahead.

Knowing the Euro Final's being recorded back at our unit I'm on high alert for any possible spoilers. No radio. No internet surfing. I want to be surprised when I watch the match.

I cover my ears as they approach and say rather loudly, "You're not talking about the soccer, are you?!"

"What?"

"Huh?"

"What?"

I uncover my ears. "You're not talking about the soccer match, the Euro Final, are you?"

They laugh, "Oh, no, no need to worry. No. We're looking for the fairy tale. Have you seen it?"

Deb and I exchange a look and shrug. "Don't think so."

"Ah, it used to be right along here. Someone populated this stretch of forest with trolls and elves. Right here along the trail. It was wonderful. But we haven't been back for years. Looks like it's gone."

"Or the trolls moved elsewhere?" I suggest.

They nod, thoughtfully. "Yes, possibly. Well, progress, I suppose."

We nod in unison, still somewhat unsure of what we're talking about, then, with smiles and waves, carry on. ❧

HUM OF SEASIDE
AND TRANSIT

Haro Strait's particularly greenish today.

From Lands End we've driven a few kilometres into town, which in this case is Sidney, a.k.a. Sidney by the Sea. WSÁNEĆ land. It's the southeast corner of Vancouver Island, toward the top of Saanich Peninsula. It's a small but busy community, and its proximity to Swartz Bay ferry terminal makes it a destination and throughway all at once.

Following our previous few weeks of relatively quiet locales, we're temporarily taken aback by the urban feel of the place. Fewer hellos on the street, the anonymity of a larger centre. But along with that comes access to a diverse array of services. You see it in professional buildings and health care providers, which speaks to demographics (an abundance of hearing and dental centres). There's a swath of bookstores – new, used, specialized and antiquarian – and I experience one of those baffling moments when a retailer's annoyed by the inconvenience of a customer wanting to buy things.

It's a pedestrian-friendly town centre, and every other passerby seems to be working on an ice cream, the vibe of a seaside tourist enclave. There's an aquarium and fish market by the water and countless shops and restaurants. Veering south, on foot, we link up with Sidney's Waterfront Walkway, a two-and-a-half-kilometre stretch of paved path that parallels the shoreline. Haro Strait is particularly greenish today, separating us from the US. The walkway's a pleasant stroll bordered in flowering hedgerows with water views of Sidney Island and Mount Baker's sky-piercing isosceles. Along the walk are benches and tables, ideal for picnics.

The walk encompasses Beacon Wharf and the Bevan Fishing Pier, where anglers toss crab traps and spin-cast. We skirt the Sidney-to-Anacortes ferry terminal and walk by a stretch of homes with well-maintained yards on Lochside Drive. Farther south the path links to a westbound shared trail for walkers and cyclists that veers toward Victoria International Airport. We're on the flight path here, and the roar of mid-sized jets passing over reminds us just how close we are to the rest of the world. ❧

SPROING!

Exuding the energy of a place undisturbed.

I've nestled the vehicle between SUVs in a parking lot, a short stroll from Sidney pier. Overhead sky resembles the sea, folds of tourmaline crested in wisps of white. With a daypack over a shoulder, we're making a watery jaunt into the strait, to Sidney Island.

We're among 20 people waiting for the foot passenger ferry: day trippers like us with small packs, as well as overnight campers loaded with water and coolers and gear. (There's no water on the island at this time.) A mom and two small kids are humping in enough kit to support a battalion: a series of duffles, packs and a wagon.

A heavy-set guy is droning on his phone, describing the features of his high-tech pack.

"Brand new. Eighty litres. Got it on sale. Two hundred bucks. Half price. Reinforced lining. The works. Hauling forty pounds of water. The rest; food, gear. Like when I was in Asia. Haul it in, haul it out. All on your back. Gotta rely on yourself."

The ferry, which is more of a water taxi, arrives to truncate the monologue, and he pushes ahead of the mom and her kids, dragging his pack behind him.

Following a brief safety announcement, the boat trundles from the pier, hauling us due east. Wind picks up from the south, raising the chop, and I'm happy to sit and enjoy a peripheral view.

Sidney Island from above resembles a turtle with its neck extending north. Its geographical high point is in the middle, a few dozen metres above sea level, and the whole has a slightly rounded look to it, further likening its appearance to that of a sea turtle. Sidney Spit is the main reason we're making the journey, a curving jut of atoll-like shore that runs alongside the island's long neck. The sand is fine, ideal for walking and beachcombing and bright enough to call white, although it's closer in colour to cream.

As our little ferry slows to dock at the island, we pass a few pleasure boats moored in the lee of the spit. One couple waves languidly from a hammock on a sailboat, the look of a lottery ad. With a slight bump we dock at the pier, and disgorge our little knot of day trippers and campers.

Perhaps it's no surprise, but the loud and self-reliant man's spouse is carrying his giant new pack loaded with water and gear. Meanwhile, he's carrying a folded map, nothing else, and arguing with no one about directions. Within moments our cluster's dispersed, and it feels as though we're alone, freshly deposited mutineers, left to survive on our own. Despite how it feels, there are currently four back-and-forth sailings each day: two in the morning and two in the afternoon, so we make a point of keeping an eye on the time as we set off to explore the island.

Once a provincial marine park, it's now part of the Gulf Islands National Park Reserve. Things are well maintained and signage is good. "Don't drink the water" warnings are prevalent. There's fine print as well. "Irrespective of boiling, the water is unsafe. If you have a heart condition, etc., etc., drinking the water can be extremely dangerous." And here I thought, "Don't drink the water" was sufficient, but I suppose the point needs to be hammered home.

There's a photocopied map of trails, the compact area making it feel easy to navigate with confidence, and we head out on a tamped-earth path through tall conifers. I thought I'd learn what I could about the island, but all I could find was the ferry schedule, real estate ads and a 136-page government report on the soil. So I now know when we need to get back to the dock, and although I've led us in the wrong direction I also know we're now traipsing over coarsely textured fluvial, or eolian material. Government-approved dirt.

The evergreens are high and exude the energy of a place undisturbed. Branches creak in the breeze and birds flit by, along with colourful moths and dragonflies. At a break in the foliage, we have a view of the beach, and less than 50 metres away an eagle stands on the shore, wings spread, ripping apart a flatfish. I'm guessing flounder, although it's doing no such thing at the moment. The eagle looks up the slope to where we are, a ribbon of sashimi dangling from its beak, as though waiting for us to move on. We oblige.

The trail cuts through an open expanse of dry grass that feels like a field of tinder, and the thought of a lighting strike or stray cigarette makes me wince. The place and conditions demand extreme caution. As we curl our way back in an oval-shaped loop, something goes *sproing* in my leg. Not that it *actually* makes that noise. The only audible sound is a grunt and a curse from me.

We slow our pace considerably and I limp my way back to the dock. We're left with a few minutes before the next boat and with shoes off we stroll the sand in the spit. A thick band of seagrass shores up the dunes, bordered in kelp and driftwood. It's a diverse swath of marine biosphere, all in a compact sliver of land. A sign warns of a seal cub nearby and to not, under any condition, tread on the grass, which pretty much holds this place together. Pebbles and small shells decorate the sand, but their miniscule size and sparseness tell me this popular bit of shore gets picked clean by beachcombers. It does, however, make for a pleasant, cushiony walk, which I'm currently doing with a bit of a lilt and a drag.

The ferry ride home in the sun with a gentle rock of waves has the lulling effect of the hammock we saw on the sailboat, a lullaby that has my head bobbing. I'm woken from my drowse by the bark of a dog. We're back at Sidney's whale watching dock, where we departed from a few hours ago, and a man and his dog, a young black lab, are here to greet two passengers. The lab's spotted the two on the boat and can't wait to see them. The rest of us chuckle as the dog literally jumps with joy. ❖

CRICKET CHIRP

---

*The smell of fresh coffee and crinkle
of morning newspaper.*

I wake to the sound of a lone cricket chirping, the
sound of dying on stage, and I get up with a smile.
"Tough crowd," I say aloud. And our day's begun.

I'm still hobbled from whatever *sproinged* in my
leg, so with an elevated foot I've assumed the role
of navigator and Deb's behind the wheel, driving us
to the ferry. From our unit on Lands End Road we're
only a kilometre from the ferry, but to access the
terminal we need to get onto Highway 17, go in the
opposite direction (south) for a few kilometres, exit,
cross four lanes, get back on the highway, then head
north to where we began.

It's early, but the sun's already high, sure to be
another hot day. The ferry line feels relaxed, with
a smell of coffee, whispered conversation and the
crinkle of newsprint, as a few dozen vehicles wait for
a series of boats. Swartz Bay, the busy terminus here
in North Saanich, is known as Victoria terminal.
As well as the ferry hauling passengers, cars and

commercial vehicles to the BC mainland, smaller craft sail to and from the Southern Gulf Islands: Salt Spring, Saturna, Pender, Galiano and Mayne, a warren of routes fanning north and east from the Saanich Peninsula.

Today we're exploring **Xʷənen'əč**. Salt Spring Island. And our ferry takes us to Fulford Harbour in the crook of a fjord like notch on Salt Spring's south side. Traffic departs and scatters somewhat, although as with any unloading there's a predominant line of cars going one way. In our case, that way is more or less north through the island's geographical centre.

This spot was first populated by Salishan Nations, with Europeans arriving in the mid-nineteenth century and renaming it Admiral Island. Notes taken during early English exploration of the area mark the island as Chuan, meaning "straight down to the sea," a Cowichan name for the mountain that commands the south of the island, now an ecological reserve. Over time Chuan morphed into Tuan, and then Tuam, a phonetical epithet the mountain retains today.

When Governor James Douglas explored these waters by canoe in the early 1850s, he felt certain the salt springs on the island "would be of the greatest importance and become a wealth to the country."

Turns out the arable land was a better economic incentive, but the governor remained a bit of a visionary, dreaming of economic expansion.

Salt Spring got its current English moniker about a hundred years ago, being the first Gulf Island populated by Europeans, and with that relative age retains a sense of establishment. Agriculture attracted more settlers, and as we drive winding, undulating roads, farmland's still prevalent alongside the woods. It's still the busiest, most populous Southern Gulf island. And as we make our way into the eastern port of Long Harbour, even on a weekday morning, the village is bustling.

Deb goes to sightsee while I limp my way through town. I've got an authorly hat on again and visit Salt Spring's inviting bookstores to sign books and take photos. Once more we're wearing masks indoors, and while masked photographs possess a touch of the clandestine, the results are uniquely revealing. Hidden are the toothy grins so often seen in photos. Instead, eyes become predominant. The shine of a radiant iris, crinkles at the corners, a warmth and intimacy I find richer than photoshop smiles. These captured moments remind me of the hongi, the shared breath ritual of the Māori, in which foreheads are pressed together. It's impossible to be perfunctory, never resembling a dismissive, limp handshake. Contact and connection are established with each and every shared meeting of eye, forehead and breath, that place we all are one.

Now, with new books and photos of warm, smiling eyes, we make our way to the centre of this northern part of the island. From an aerial perspective the land mass resembles a bee: three meaty chunks like a head, thorax and abdomen, with inlets that squeeze in the narrow parts. Behind us is Long Harbour, while across the island, facing Crofton on Big Island, is Salt Spring's alternate ferry terminal at Vesuvius Bay.

For lunch we drive up a hill to a cidery set in the trees. In fact, it's a clearing amidst an arid expanse of forest. The island's virtually out of water for now, a dilemma that seems to recur every year. Fire bans are in effect, the danger level extreme, and this pap of land enshrouded in evergreen feels like dehydrated Eden.

We order share plates of food and a taster flight of ciders: dry apple, sweet, scrumpy, grapefruit and pear. Small, ornate glasses are set in a row on a rough handled wood tray, the look of a removable toolbox rack. Food pairings are recommended, and a sequence in which they're supposed to be drunk. But it's hot and I'm thirsty and the little bubbly drinks simply go down as I reach for them. I'm not one for cider, but the setting's ideal, fruit orchards spilling down the hill, and with a feeling of "when in Rome," the overall experience is a good one.

Just as in the unrushed process of fermentation, food gets prepared at a leisurely pace and served when it's served. There's no point in hurrying, and we settle into the pace of the kitchen and patrons. I scan the surrounding picnic tables, some in the sun, others in umbrella shade. Guests return for refills. Books are being read. A cribbage board comes out. It feels like a respite from the hum of the rest of the island and those who are here embrace it.

Three overdressed women arrive, scan the environment, take selfies and leave. I wonder what they'll lie about on their food blogs, and realize five tiny glasses of cider render me a cynic.

Following lunch, we drive south toward the island's abdomen and I peel back another layer of local history, which took place shortly after Governor Douglas paddled through, envisioning a future when Salt Spring would rival the spas of Bath. In addition to those first Europeans, African-American settlers came here, fleeing anti-Black legislation in California. Apparently, Governor Douglas was pro-immigration, and let it be known people in these parts would be treated fairly. Hmm. ♣

A FROG NAMED STEVE

A richer life because of that presence.

Our new accommodation, here in Quw'utsun, the Cowichan Valley, is at Shawnigan Lake. And is, in fact, new. A freshly converted garage with posh bathroom, the unit surrounded in greenery. Outside, on a small patio, the neighbour's cherry-plum tree hangs into our yard, offering shade in purple leaves and fresh, juicy fruit in matching deep colour.

A resident tree frog comes to visit, enjoying the cool shade of a storage container used for outdoor seat cushions. To my surprise the little frog leaps into my hand, turning me into a 12-year-old. That was the age I was when I got a small African tree frog as a pet, one of a few to surface at our local pet shop, a novelty we assumed was part of an order gone wrong. It stayed in a fishbowl of water on my dresser, floating at the surface to breathe while living mostly underwater, wedged between rocks. It ate frog food. Yes, the pet store had frog food, tiny cylindrical pellets the colour of loam.

I named him Steve. I believe Steve identified as he/him/his because he croaked (not slang for passed away but *actually* croaked), and I learned only males of the species croak. By the time I left home to go to university, Steve had been my pet for eight years. People were surprised at how long I'd had him.

"How long do they live?" they'd ask. To which I'd shrug. I imagined Steve would be part of my life as long as was intended; no more, no less.

Fitting neatly in the base of a cupped hand, he had a peaty-green back, cream-coloured belly and the quads of a skater. Every so often he'd let out his high-pitched croak, a kind of clicking. *Click...click.* Occasionally, he'd double down. *Click-click...click-click.* It sounded like two small rocks being tapped together or someone striking a flint. I could make him stop by resting my finger against the side of his bowl. A simple relationship really, but Steve was a great pet, bringing fun and consistency to my life, and I liked to believe he was better off having one square meal a day in a small but safe environment, far from his traditional African predators. (There hadn't been a leopard or hyena sighting in Vernon, BC, for as long as I could remember.)

Steve and I went to university. The first time, we drove. I was at the wheel, Steve in a travel jar (a one-quart Mason). Later, we flew, Steve once more in his travel Mason. This was pre-9/11. And as I slid Steve, jar and all, through the security X-ray system along with my keys and wallet, airport security, a seemingly competent, youngish woman let out a lung-splitting, Hollywood horror film scream! More security materialized, a few heavily armed. The shrieker, I felt, lacked the cool professionalism the role warrants. However. Things simmered down, somewhat. Along with explanations. Apologies. Then grins and chuckles.

"How long do they live?"

Shrug.

Steve and I managed to make our flight and ended up having a pleasant journey. There was no meal option for Steve as he was on my lap, flying free. Like a toddler, only cuter.

Six years later, Steve and I headed off to grad school, a 4000-kilometre drive. Late on the third day I was stopped for speeding. It was starless dark and the officer used a flashlight to approach our car. I had my licence out. Steve was on the dash in his Mason jar. The officer didn't seem to notice me, his flashlight trained on Steve.

"You transporting live bait?" a voice asked from behind the light. The beam stayed on Steve and I wasn't sure who was being addressed. The question was repeated. Steve remained silent, so I did the talking.

"Well, no, officer," I said. "Just my pet frog. His name's Steve." (I figured a first-name basis might break the ice.)

"Where you coming from?"

I told him.

"There's been a rash of Dutch elm disease through here," he said.

Which sounded somewhat accusatory, so I thought I'd better defuse the situation. "Oh, no problem there, officer. We're not Dutch." Then for some reason I added, "And never have been."

I wasn't sure what to make of the quiet emanating from the mix of dark and blinding light.

Turned out the elm disease was a regional epidemic and simply a conversation starter. The silence was broken by the sound of a freshly written ticket being torn from the pad. The officer passed it to me with a smile and wished the two of us a safe drive.

$75. For a late night visit and a decent story. I felt that was fair.

Two years later Steve and I finished grad school. (Truth be told, I did the work. He just swam and partied, somehow managing to join a fraternity.) We came home, I started a job and Steve got back to his regimen of laps, mealtime and occasional croaks. I felt he was aging.

A year later, after having been my pet for 17 years (we don't know how old he was when I got him),

Steve passed away. I'd still have to explain him to people. Usually with a shrug. Questions arose and the novelty of Steve seemed to last. Silly, maybe, but Steve was an important part of my life. He was there for my adolescence, growing up, college, university, relationships and jobs. In the same way I'd put a finger to his bowl to calm his croaking, Steve was a touchstone, a reassuring constant while every other facet of life changed. A richer life, I believe, because of that presence. ❖

AROMA OF OYSTERS

An exodus, people moving in all directions.

A short drive from **Shawnigan Lake** and we're in
Mill Bay, ferry terminal for the back-and-forth
sailing to Brentwood Bay on the Saanich Penin
sula. The strip mall servicing Mill Bay reminds me
of a magician, a never ending stream of stuff spilling
from a hat. The mall snakes around a seemingly
compact space but magically offers up every retail
and professional service imaginable. Although the
area lacks a defined town centre, every amenity is
here. I pick up the free local newspaper at one of the
supermarkets (the editorial room is next door) and
decide I could live quite comfortably in this little
dent in the coast, facing the Saanich Inlet.

We go for brunch at a resto-pub on the Mill Bay
pier. Mount Baker cuts a dramatic outline on the
horizon, snow-capped blue on blue. Tide's out and
everything smells of oysters. A clump of patrons are
lined up at the door to the pub, signage the same as
in restaurants everywhere. "Sorry, shortened hours
due to lack of staff." Another place had a billboard,
"Now hiring: dishwasher, line cook, kitchen staff

and servers." In other words, anyone and everyone required to run a restaurant. It's an ongoing spill-over of the effects of COVID. Later, we'd hear much the same thing from a hiker on one of the trails. "It's an exodus. People are moving, in all directions." ❧

INTO THE TREES

A view through arbutus and pine.

Shawnigan Lake is indigo, calm and speckled with morning sunlight. We hop in the car and drive toward rising sun, to Cobble Hill, cross two sets of train tracks and park at a network of trailheads in Cobble Hill Mountain Regional Recreation Area. It's a diverse expanse of shared trails for hikers, mountain bikes and horseback riding, with gentle woodsy strolls and steep, demanding climbs. Trails are well marked with colour-coded signs that correspond to what I know from ski hills: green is easy, blue moderate and black routes are challenging. We try a blend of each to summit the hill, a few hundred metres of elevation, our reward a view through arbutus and pine to the north tip of Saanich Peninsula.

Another couple summits shortly after us, a woman and man who savour the view and strike up conversation.

"Whew! Underestimated that distance," he says.

"Took the long way today," she adds.

"Which way did you come?" I ask.

He turns and sweeps his arm in a wide arc behind him. "From the bottom we came up the next valley over, behind this ridge. Completely cut off from this breeze. No trees!" He gulps some water. "I couldn't believe how different the land is. Just over there. All dry. Totally different."

"Yeah," she adds. "Thankfully, no kids today. They complain all the way!" she laughs. "Fourteen and eleven. They'd rather be on their Game Boys. Nonstop grumble, grumble, grumble." She laughs again. "But you know, as long as they're talking, they've got the wind for it. Plenty of energy!"

We visit a while longer. It turns out they're local, and they give us a few recommendations for sightseeing and meal options, their laughter and company a pleasant addition to the hike. The four of us spend a few quiet minutes taking in the vast view, treed slopes, a stretch of sea and, beyond that, the easterly edge of Big Island, glinting in blistering sun. ❖

SQUIRREL, FROG, TURTLE AND ELK

Watching a whole lot of nothing go by.

Today we're back to climb Cobble Hill, starting the day with a few of the green routes to the summit. In addition to a grading colour, each trail has a corresponding animal marker. Today we go from Squirrel to Frog, and carry on to Turtle. This is what we tried last time but wound up on an Elk, which led us to a road.

Across the tracks from the trailhead sits Olde School Coffee, a former school and now a busy coffee and food spot. The building's two storeys in fire engine red, and still looks the part of an early twentieth-century schoolhouse. Monstrous fir trees sit at the corners of the lot, throwing shade on a few picnic tables.

Dusty and hungry, we head in for post-hike breakfast. The coffeehouse is in the basement, and descending into the space I'm teleported back to my high school cafeteria. Identical, I'm sure, to school lunchrooms everywhere. Mrs. M would be tossing mini-pizzas onto baking sheets each morning like frozen Frisbees, and from our homeroom, adjacent to the lunchroom, we'd pop in to see what was on offer, thinking it might be something other than pizza. It never was.

Now, with Americanos and breakfast sandwiches in hand, we sit among dry pine needles, the scent of evergreen and fresh coffee clinging agreeably, and watch a whole lot of nothing go by. This area, part of the Cowichan Valley, is famous for forestry and farming. The agriculture is diverse and abundant, producing fruit, vegetables and meat. The local museum speaks to this, with farmstead history and old photos of massive trees felled in the previous century.

I get a feel for the time from a series of black and white snapshots of loaded logging trucks in the 1940s, taken in Bellingham, due east of us in Washington state. One photo shows a logging truck "train," a dozen trucks, each loaded to capacity with a single piece of gargantuan log. What was being felled must've been hundreds of years old. Setting aside, for a moment, the sentiment toward old-growth logging, the engineering required was remarkable. Difficult, demanding and dangerous work that drove economies across the island and mainland for decades. Gazing at the photographs I feel I'm standing at a cenotaph, fallen logs like un-named soldiers, lives given, perhaps, for something more. And I give them a minute of silence. ❧

E & N Line, Qualicum to Parksville

Blacktail Doe and Fawn, Saanich Peninsula

Swartz Bay to Tsawwassen Ferry

A Frog Named Steve

800-Year-Old Douglas Fir, Qualicum

SNOWBIRDS
AND ICE CREAM

The roar melds with the sound of the sea.

Today we've made a leisurely drive north from Shawnigan to Cowichan Bay, once more on the east coast of Big Island. At first I wonder what's going on, as the narrow road into town is lined with cars, down the sloping road into the village centre, all the way through, petering out somewhere beyond a boat launch. But it turns out this is just the way it is, here in "Cow Bay." The little community simply seems to bulge at the seams. I can't imagine what they do when it's actually busy here. Because it *is* a destination. An eclectic strip of independent, creative shops front the road: art, gifts, a bakery, a candy shop and ice cream maker, a perfumery, a café, a restaurant and a steady stream of tourists, armed with ice cream cones and stumbling into traffic. Locals dodge their way through, getting on with life, which centres around the dock and marina, commercial and sport fishing along with recreational boating. Water-based tours depart from here as well. It feels like the end of the road, although the seaside route carries on toward Duncan, a relaxed alternative to the highway inland.

We buy bread and fragrances (as you do). My scent was analyzed by the perfumer and apparently my natural aroma is that of the Carmanah Valley (old-growth rainforest). And here I'd thought it was old socks and Mennen. Now, smelling strongly of moss, I line up for double scoop cones of local handmade ice cream, which is some of the best we've had. We find a bench in maple shade and enjoy a marina view, set back from the busyness of the shops. A dog walker stops to say hello as their Pomeranian poos at our feet. We return friendly nods and move on.

On our way back to the vehicle we hear a low rumble, which grows, the thunder of military jets. We're now in an open patch of land by the water and the tightly packed, nine-plane formation of the Canadian Forces Snowbirds screams past, low and directly overhead, bearing due north. We discover it's in response to the COVID pandemic, and while making for a superb display, it strikes me as a terribly expensive reminder to wash your hands and get vaccinated. But I learn it's, in fact, Operation Inspiration, a cross-Canada aerial tour to "salute front-line healthcare workers, first responders, essential workers, and all Canadians doing their part to stop the spread of COVID-19." The jets bank east behind Salt Spring and vanish, but long after they're gone their roar echoes, melding with the thrum of the sea. ❖

WHEN TURKEYS CROSS THE ROAD

We eat here four times in 12 days.

Tonight we're dining in Shawnigan Lake (the town, that is, not the body of water). We're at The Corner Table, a charming eatery run by the spousal chef team of Carrie and Chris. Carrie's from South Korea, Chris from Ontario. They met at culinary school here on Vancouver Island and started their restaurant a few years ago. The menu's small and changes frequently, with ingredients locally sourced. The two do the job of a full kitchen staff, and they do it well. We end up eating here four times in 12 days.

Chris comes out from the kitchen for a visit, and at that moment a few wild turkeys saunter across the road.

"Makes you think, right?" Deb says, smiling.

"You mean *why* they cross the road?" Chris says with a grin.

"I was thinking more like when you're planning the menu."

"Yeah," Chris laughs. "When I was working on the place, building this deck, they'd walk right through the restaurant, hang out for a while then wander away."

"And you never wanted to...?"

"Well, sure, it crossed my mind. But, nah! Too tough, I'm sure."

And we chuckle as the turkeys meander by, give us a dirty look and carry on into the woods. ❖

FLY RODS AND LILIES

A gift without an occasion.

Seated on a deck, we're dining al fresco at a pub with a new view of Shawnigan Lake, our vantage point a small, well-treed cove. Sun's setting through thick old cedar and the ambience is superb. A couple dining next to us have arrived by boat. Down the slope from where we are, the lake surface looks bejewelled. A houseboat burbles away from shore and a raft of flowering lilies blankets the shallows in buttercup yellow and green.

"Lily pads!" I say a bit too loudly, and point.

The visual takes me again to adolescence, fishing in lakes like this, outsized blue dragonflies skimming the water, as Dad and I would position ourselves at the perimeter of lily pad beds to fly-cast for trout. When the pads were in bloom it felt extra special, a gift without an occasion.

Of course, there was an added element of acumen required to cast *up to* the lilies, not into them. Our thinking being that's where the biggest fish ought to be. I suppose it added to the fun as well, like throwing darts, imagining savvy and skill would trump luck and feeding cycles we never did bother to learn. All I know is it was a feeling of immersion in nature, the conjoining of flora and fauna. Although I didn't yet know those words, I comprehended just the same. And then those exhilarating moments a fish struck and ran, the *whzzz* of fly line on reel, doing our best to coax scaled quarry from the line-knotting wrath of the tubers. *That's* what I feel, connection and adrenalized memories, any time I see lilies on water. ❧

MID-ISLAND ISLANDS

——————

A raptor circles a thin crescent moon.

This morning we're in **Campbell River.** Wiwek'a̱m. Two and a half hours north of Shawnigan, once more on Big Island's east side. I've climbed a small urban hill where an unruly blackberry bush bursts with fresh fruit. I fill a container, about two punnets' worth, and make my way back to our current home, a small apartment above a garage. It's not even nine in the morning and it's already 30 degrees Celsius.

Down the hill I have a sea view, through Japanese maple, mountain ash and a monkey puzzle tree, of the strait separating us from Quadra Island, which today resembles a tree-topped submarine with a communications tower that could be a periscope. I can just make out its lighthouse off to the south. Overhead sky's cloudless, summertime blue, with a lone raptor circling a thin crescent moon. Passing vehicles seem to be moving slowly. Maybe it's the heat. It's a weekday but a weekday in summer, and everything seems half speed.

Tugboats amble through the strait, dragging barges and oddly shaped structures on floats, mobile maritime cranes and frameworks for some sort of industrial construction happening somewhere up the strait. They'll burble and bob their way north of town, past Tyee Spit, where a small grassy park sits beside what was once the world's busiest float plane terminal. Anglers take centre stage here, as it's home to the Tyee Club of BC. Tyee is a Chinook Nuu-chah-nulth word used to describe a spring salmon exceeding 30 pounds (about 14 kilos).

To earn a spot in this hundred-year-old fishing club you need to catch a Tyee Chinook salmon following a strict set of rules: your boat must be paddled or rowed, your lure artificial with barbless hook, your monofilament fishing line strength no more than 20 pounds. In other words, it's a fair fight. Off the shore of the spit, crisply white rowboats bob on the chop, craft that belong in Hyde Park with parasols and poetry. The smart money here's on the salmon.

Exploring town on foot, we hug the shoreline and follow the six-kilometre Rotary Seawalk, admiring chainsaw carvings of eagles, salmon and salt-seasoned mariners. Forestry and fishing have driven the economy here for years, with Campbell River considered the salmon capital of the world. The beach is a blend of sea-smoothed gravel and bowling ball rocks, a few paddling mallards and scaups, with a screeching cluster of monochrome Bonaparte's gulls.

Back at the unit, I visit with our temporary land-lord, a local realtor.

"We don't have time for open houses," he says. "Things are selling too quickly."

"Is it still industry?" I ask.

He nods. "And people moving from elsewhere."

Once again, the familiar sentiment. *People moving, in all directions.* ❧

THE DAY WITH
THE CLOUD

When the runway smouldered like a war zone.

Another hot, cloudless morning, of which we've had 45 in a row. One day had a scuff of overcast and became a topic of conversation.

"Remember that day?"

"The one with the cloud?"

"Yeah!"

Here on the islands we've been mercifully removed from wildfires across BC. A few days of eerily stunning sunlight but nothing like we experienced in the Okanagan in the noughties. I'd flown into Kelowna Airport as hills either side of the runway smouldered like a war zone. I'd been arranging house insurance for our newly built home. The conversation with the insurance agent went something like this.

"Where exactly is the property?" she asked.

"You know where the fires are?" I said.

"Um, yes."

"Right there."

" ... "

Unlike others, we were fortunate. Our home got built, insured and (as far as I know) is still standing.

Acquaintances told me of having to flee their home in Okanagan Mission at the time and watching the evening news, live, from a relative's home, as fire raged beside the house they'd fled, engulfing their next door neighbours' home. Then the broadcast cut back to the newsroom.

They went through the stages of grief, they explained, then came around to the notion of rebuilding. They felt fortunate no one was hurt, and before long were excited about the new home they'd design with the insurance proceeds. But the fire, they learned, had jumped their house, leaving it untouched. And they admitted, following all those emotions, and the acceptance and eventual excitement of new plans, they were disappointed their home was intact. ✤

HIKE WITH A SEAL

Forest thick with fern and salal.

A long weekend is upon us and we're sticking to Big Island, avoiding busy holiday routes. Camper vans and trucks with trailers in tow are heading to ferry terminals, but we're keeping to the slow lane, hugging the island's east coast and making our way south from Campbell River to Seal Bay Nature Park, part of the Comox Valley Regional District. There's a gravel car park and trailheads either side of the road. Some paths are shared – horses, bikes and hikers – but the network's extensive, and even on a stat holiday we soon find ourselves on our own. Two looping seaside trails weave through healthy second-growth forest, thick with fern and salal. Paths are groomed gravel and spongy dirt, the kind you can walk on all day. Despite the heat, tall trees and sea breeze keep us comfortably cool. Trails weave atop a ravine and a spur track takes us down a steep embankment to the water. Bleached driftwood marks the tideline where a rocky shore curves into bay. The water has the fresh saline scent of being far from humanity. A leafy deciduous canopy provides resort-like umbrellas, and I feel like Robinson Crusoe. Or Alexander Selkirk. Which I mention solely to sound well read.

Even through the wavering shade of trees and thick SPF we soon feel ourselves shift from medium-rare to well-done and drag ourselves up the steep trail to resume a level and leisurely loop back to the vehicle. Total seal sightings at the park: one. A slick-headed harbour seal watching from a distance. I like to believe somewhere in the depths the seal too is keeping a journal. "Total people sightings at the beach: two. A good-looking one and her mate, scribbling in a notebook of tree-gut and cow." (My journal's covered in *imitation* cow, mind you, but there's no way the seal could know that from that distance.)

A low rumble fills the sky, the vibration of nearing thunder, and a fighter jet screams overhead, its throaty roar the kind that forces you to cover your ears and wonder how much damage is being done to your hearing. Canadian Forces Base Comox is directly south of us and what just passed over, I believe, is a CF-18 Hornet. The airfield accommodates both military and commercial air traffic. The base, also known as 19 Wing Comox, houses Comox Air Force Museum, and as we drive past a short while later we slow for a gawking glimpse at coastal patrol planes and a monstrous tandem-rotor transport helicopter used for search and rescue. The kind every Tom Clancy character has to leap from at some point to save the world yet again. ✿

HERE ON THE COAST

Waterlogged wood, bending time.

From **Seal Bay Nature Park** we drive around the Comox peninsula to Balmoral Beach and Goose Spit Park, where the water's a ripple of gems on tinfoil. A wall of seasoned grey timber, logs standing on end, has been planted to shore up the beach. The reinforcement looks like a frontier fort, defence against fierce winter storms.

Even though it's been a long day, I want to avoid the Inland Island Highway 19, so instead opt for the slower, meandering Old Island Highway 19A, the Oceanside Route. Last time I was here I used both roadways, alternating between inland and coast, stopping at bookstores to sign books and visit with readers. It became a road trip and book tour, promoting *Gone Viking: A Travel Saga* and *Gone Viking II: Beyond Boundaries*. Both titles won some awards, and the sequel had just hit retailers' shelves.

I'd made a point of lingering here, this K'ómoks region another unique part of Big Island, Coast Salish having fished the Courtenay River Estuary for four millennia. The climate is good, the soil ideal for crops, and marine life's abundant. Indigenous locals called these parts kw'umuxws, meaning plentiful. With anglicization the name became Komoux, precursor to present-day Comox.

On my previous drive through, the estuary was particularly picturesque, an expanse of lush river side greens surrounding sun-dappled blue. I stopped the car for a landscape photo, and it was as though I captured a painting. From my vantage point on the side of the road I could see most of the estuary, where original inhabitants set complex networks of weirs, nets affixed to stakes to catch fish at high tide. When water receded twice daily, harvesting occurred. The weir stakes are visible at low tide, and I could see quite a few. Archaeologists have counted hundreds of thousands of them here, carved from hemlock, up to 3,000 years old, and I wondered which ones I saw, waterlogged wood bending time.

Now, the town of Comox feels like a sleepy kid sibling with Courtenay the still-growing teen. At a Comox bookstore the owner explained how quiet it is, even in the heart of town. Driving in did indeed feel like another time warp. Not in terms of millennia, but decades, with old-style light standards, shops fronting a narrow street, with summertime blooms in planters. It felt like my hometown of Vernon when I was a boy. You would know shop owners' names, and they likely knew yours. There was always someone sweeping out front, offering up a wave. Then again, I may be confusing childhood memories with old TV shows. Regardless, present-day Comox is pleasant and peaceful.

Courtenay, on the other hand, is busy. A larger, denser population than Comox. Big box retailers. Traffic. A place to make a living, perhaps, for career-minded workers. I know a number of folks who've moved from Vancouver to here. Known as "halfers," they sell their homes in the city, bank half and use the remaining half to buy an equivalent home on Big Island. They're happy, and do well by it. It does, however, drive up prices where they find their new homes. If I were saving for a place around here, I imagine it'd be easy to resent the "come-from-aways," but of course we could say that about anywhere, as far back as we care to go.

Here in Courtenay I visit with Evelyn, owner of Laughing Oyster Bookshop, her storefront a welcoming rainbow splash of flowers. Another round of signing books, then I buy some new titles to add to my own stack of volumes to read. I pick up Howard White's *Here on the Coast*, and grin as I flip through a passage: "BC Coast people are joined by certain things universal to the region: a weary resignation to living with rain and BC Ferries, a familiarity with gumboots, bumbershoots, rain slicks, life jackets, seagull droppings, barnacle lacerations, antifouling paint, disappearing fish, disappearing forests," which I find myself silently reading with an affably cantankerous voice, one that can't help but love the place being talked about. I learn that a bumbershoot's an umbrella, and later, when Deb lacerates a foot on a barnacle, I let her know the good news, that she's officially BC Coast people. ✤

THE ROAD AND
RED DRESSES

A sound of place and land and people.

Now in **Campbell River,** we've ventured into Beaver Lodge Forest Lands, a 400-hectare expanse of trees and public footpaths with rocky streambeds, now mostly dry. Drought-like conditions are prevalent, and here, as elsewhere, there are fire bans. Water restrictions are also in place and lawns are scorched and yellow. This patch of forest is unique in that nearly a century ago it was donated to the province by Elk River Timber Company, in trust, for experimental reforestation work. It had been logged by railway and was reforested through plantings and natural regeneration, making it the first operational plantation of its kind in BC to be legislatively protected, and is now a popular public destination for walkers, cyclists and horseback riders. Thick foliage and a gentle undulation dampens the hum of nearby roadways, and it's another fine way to start another fine day.

Our little home for now faces east, and today's morning sun is, as they say, dancing on the water. Seriously. It could be a samba. Past the rhythmic glint of water, Quadra has a hogback look about it, down to a bristly forest outline. Beyond that are the craggy blue peaks of the mainland's Coast Mountains. This current accommodation is neatly positioned between two parks: Coronation and Centennial. The trees in quiet little Coronation Park appear the right age to have been planted when Elizabeth II took the throne, but no one seems to know for sure. Trees decorate the space in a tidy ring, the look of an evergreen crown. Centennial Park, on the other hand, is an energetic plot of hillside and community centre: a children's play area, swimming pool and tennis courts where seniors smack pickleballs, the unmistakable noise of Wiffle ball plastic being hammered in flight, a sound I associate with active retirement.

A stroll up the hill to a school (closed for the summer) puts me back in the thicket of blackberries, where I feast once more like a bear preparing for winter. A grass field's bordered in mesh fence, decorated with flat, hand-painted eagles in wood – 200 pieces of art – the fingerprint swirls of creative students and open minds.

Back atop the garage, I refill the hummingbird mug with coffee and spend time simply thinking, remembering a particular day on the road. A day in which radio stations dedicated airtime to First Nations, Indigenous locals sharing their stories and talking. Each story, a few minutes long, honest, heart-wrenching and hopeful. I listened to a man tell his story of hiding as a child beneath a vehicle, hoping it wouldn't crush him, as his siblings were dragged away to a residential school. And a woman told the story of her sister, whom she lost, and asked for people to listen, nothing more. While a young woman from the north performed a throat-singing piece, the mesmerizing, connecting sound of place and land and people.

With soaring birds, forest and seaside, each day on the road takes us past endless red dresses, hanging from fences, overpass concrete, tree limbs and post boxes, symbols of blood, anger and love, honouring the spirits of missing and murdered Indigenous women and girls. There are more than I'm able to count. And not for the first or last time, Deb and I drive in silence. And cry. ❧

ISLAND HOPPING

A thick line of driftwood in amber and white.

"Just to Quadra?" the ticket seller asks through the window of the drive-up booth, to which I nod. Some of the vehicles queued for the ferry from Campbell River will make this into a two-sailing jaunt from Vancouver Island to Quadra and on to Cortes Island. This is the Discovery Passage, joining the Salish Sea and surrounding Discovery Islands. We're one of only a few vehicles awaiting the early morning sailing. A sleepy energy blankets the space as low sun peers from beyond our destination. The name Quadra comes from Juan Francisco de la Bodega y Quadra, the Spanish explorer from Lima who navigated these parts for Spain in the eighteenth century. And I decide (yet again) that I too would like a half dozen words to my name.

It's an easy ten-minute crossing and we disembark onto a narrow access ramp at Quathiaski Cove. We Wai Kai Nation land. Turning right, we drive through forest and farms to Quadra Island's south end, to Cape Mudge, home to a squat red and white lighthouse. A chattering family has arrived ahead of us, snapping photos and complaining about the cold. It's in the low twenties Celsius, but an onshore breeze makes it seem cooler, and they're gone a few minutes later, leaving the lighthouse and what seems like the entire south of the island to no one but us.

The beach here is a thick line of driftwood, bits of timber ranging from scaly pieces of bark to whole trees, polished to amber and white by sun, surf and time. A band of seaweed sits beneath the blanched wood, littered with tiny red crabs, now dead and dry, a dusting of crustacean confetti, while fist-sized rocks cover the rest of the beach.

I'd watched a nature show filmed here and now know a surprising number of marine fossils are found in these rocks, amongst the shale and harder, boulder-like bits called concretions. Ammonites are fairly common, the ancient cephalopod swirls that are ancestors of nautili. The guy on TV made it look easy, picking up a rock from the endless supply and whacking it with a rock hammer, resulting in the stone neatly splitting in two to reveal a compartmented swirl of cetaceous art.

Which triggered a memory from when I took a geology course in college, a course I didn't take seriously and, obviously, didn't work at. On the day of our final exam, I sat at a desk, unprepared as usual, hoping for the best. *How hard could it be?* I knew quartz and granite and fool's gold. How many other rocks could there possibly be? I figured I could bumble my way to a passing grade. For multiple choice questions, I knew when in doubt, guess "C." Not sure why, but there was consensus amongst my generation that "C" was almost always the correct answer, something teachers were unaware of but we students were convinced was true, agreeing to keep it to ourselves. Plus, in a pinch I could always fill in the short answer section with a joke. "You rock!" Or something similar. Bonus marks and a cheerful disposition were how I got through most of my courses.

The instructor set a blank exam paper in front of me, then emptied a drawstring bag of 12 identical rocks onto my desk that tumbled into a rattling, dusty heap.

"Identify these," he said.

"I think you've mistakenly given me all the same ones," I said.

He smiled, thinking I was displaying my usual attempt at wit, which I wasn't. And he *hadn't* made a mistake, of course. Two awkward hours later I accepted an F and a signed promise to the instructor I would never pursue a career in geology. It turns out there *are* quite a few different types of rock, which I now know.

I also now know these island shores are a favourite destination for fossil hunters, although samples are harder to find without a guide or a more remote locale. So for now we're simply enjoying a quiet morning amongst the anonymous rocks on south Quadra, watching sunlight brighten the lighthouse. In the strait, recreational fishing boats have begun to muster. The tide's turning, slack to flood, and a surge of chop bisects the narrows in a rising blade of white water, a vertical division of sea. ❧

KAY DUBOIS AND PETROGLYPHS

Conifers, fir, cedar and spruce,
smelling of seaside and pine.

From Quadra's southern tip we drive a bit north and east, to the end of the road. There's a muddy pullout where two compact cars can park side by side. From here we push through a network of ground cover to pick up the Kay Dubois Trail, named for a local resident, a four-kilometre out-and-back path that snakes along the coast then veers inland through high conifers, thick barked fir, scaly spruce and cedar that looks like it's due for a wallpaper makeover, all of it smelling of seaside and pine.

A short distance from the trailhead a colossal old spruce stands like a wizard guarding the forest. And, in fact, it might be, something from the past assuming the shape of a tree, captured in a conjurer's spell. It has a hundred arms, the look of a mythical god reaching every which way, one of those feats of nature impossible to capture in a photo. Perhaps in a large enough canvas. A near-audible hum surrounds the venerable beast, and I savour the space and sensation, remembering the trees from my childhood yard. The feeling of age and earthy connection no different than Dad's 60-year-old ponderosas and a baby blue spruce that he raised.

Back in the vehicle, a looping zigzag takes us across the island and gradually northeast, where we park and stroll the shoreline of Rebecca Spit Marine Provincial Park and We Wai Kai Campsite, a treed finger of land that forms part of Drew Harbour and Heriot Bay, ferry port for the Quadra-Cortes run. From the sandy shore of the spit, we watch a chubby ferry trundle by, the visual something from a children's book.

As well as fossils, this southern part of the island is home to petroglyphs, about a hundred over a dozen different sites. Petroglyph Way leads to the coast we're on now, while other viewing sites can be reached from Nuyumbalees Cultural Centre. The rock art ranges from 2,500 to 3,500 years old and includes a face chiselled into stone, hand-drilled dots in the shape of an owl and a painted visage imposed on a vibrant sun.

From the southeast of the island, we meander our way to SouthEnd Farm Winery, where we cobble together a picnic of meat, cheese and *rosé*, with a view of vineyards, butterflies and pollinating bees. Rather than cork, bottles are conveniently topped with levered stoppers, allowing samplers like us to take opened bottles home. It feels a bit like a fairytale orchard, the hum of bees and butterfly flits in yellow, pale blue and orange. I watch for a moment through the glass of blush wine and the whole becomes a rainbow, rounded in lemony sun. ❖

Fishing Weirs, Courtenay River, Comox

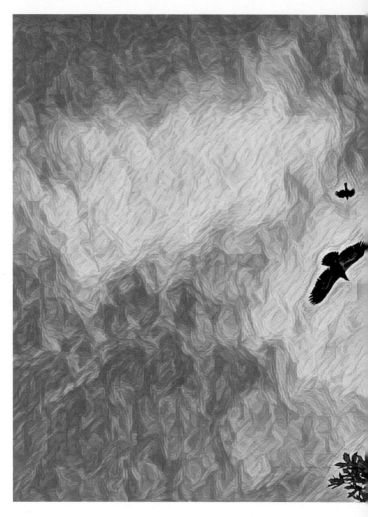

Crow and Juvenile Bald Eagle, Mid Island

Quadra Island, from Campbell River

Latitude Fifty, Campbell River

Cape Mudge Lighthouse, Quadra Island

THE BLAST
AT RIPPLE ROCK

---

*Nettles pre-bloom, with puffballs
bending in breeze.*

Back on **Big Island,** we're up with the sun, on a
trail by seven. We've driven north from Campbell River, Ligwiłdaxw land, across a bridge and over
the city's namesake, an angler in hip waders already
in the current, casting for salmon. On the outskirts
of town, a few car dealerships and an uninterrupted
stretch of curvy, high-speed road.

Pulling from the highway, we navigate a pre-
carious, lumpy stretch of gravel, briefly bottoming
out as though off-roading a safari track, working to
keep tires on high ridges between ditches. From the
scrubby patch of car park we traipse away on more
gravel, descending through wildflowers in yellow
and purple, nettles pre-bloom and dandelions in
seed, downy puffballs bending in breeze. The trail
plunges into trees, a trek of undulation, rock, dirt
and spongy deadfall, with occasional glimpses of
Discovery Passage away to our right. This is Ripple

Rock Trail, a mildly demanding, eight-kilometre out-and-back that takes us to a high plateau viewpoint of the Seymour Narrows.

Ripple Rock is a rise in the seabed, a submerged, twin-peaked mountain. Treacherous eddies decorate the surface in Charybdis swirls, but nothing compared to what it once was, when standing waves marked the unique maritime geology. This is a critical commercial waterway, hazardous for as long as it's been navigated. Captain George Vancouver was the first European to write of the area, describing it as "one of the vilest stretches of water in the world." To navigate, sure, but a stunning vista for sightseers.

In the mid-nineteenth century, plans were proposed to connect Vancouver Island to the mainland here, utilizing Ripple Rock as part of the bridge-span. But like every bridge-building proposal, it met with a flurry of political controversy matching the angst of the waterway churning beneath. Over the next century, a hundred ships sank or were irreparably damaged plying these narrows. The bridge-building contingent were eventually silenced as opinion turned, the new consensus being to blow up the rock. (Blow it up *real good*, as they'd say on SCTV). But through the 1940s, repeated efforts to destroy the rock failed. Explosive charges were laid, drilled into the rock, floated, dropped by cable – a decade's worth of Wile E. Coyote attempts to obliterate the thing – to no avail. And like the Road Runner sticking its tongue out with a scoffing *meep-meep*, Ripple Rock prevailed. Until the 1950s, when scientists at last knew how to blow things up *real good*.

From 1955 to 1958, over 150 metres of vertical shaft were drilled into nearby Maud Island, followed by 700 metres of horizontal shaft into the base of Ripple Rock, along with two more vertical shafts up into the twin peaks. From these, a series of notches called (to my delight) "coyote" shafts were drilled to accommodate the explosives, approximately 1300 metric tonnes worth. For fans of detonation, blowing things up underwater requires ten times the explosive needed on dry land. The chemical compound used was Nitramex 2H.

The RCMP cleared the area within a five-kilometre radius. A bunker was constructed for the engineers and a CBC film crew, who broadcast the event live. International scientists and bomb makers were also in attendance, eager to witness the event (and take notes). Detonation occurred on the morning of April 5, 1958. Over 600,000 metric tonnes of rock and sea were displaced in the blast, throwing debris 300 metres into the air to rain down on either side of the narrows. This resulted in an underwater clearing of roughly 14 metres, enough for even the largest ships to pass with sufficient care and timing of the tide. It remains the largest ever man-made non-nuclear explosion, and is a Canadian National Historic Event.

To get to the viewpoint at the end of the trail, some climbing's required, a satisfying hike that ensures we've earned a proper breakfast (or two). One short but steep ascent has a fixed-rope handhold strung between cliff-hugging evergreen roots. Our reward, a stunning view of the passage where the explosion took place.

Two other hikers arrive and we visit at the trail's end (the out-and-back halfway point). It's a mom and her daughter, and their English accents are strong.

"Are you from the north of the country?" I ask.

The mom smiles. "Well, north of the Midlands, yes, Sheffield."

And we chat flight paths and how one can get here from there. It's never easy, just a matter of which series of Inconveniences you choose to embrace.

"Last time we did this hike with my two kids," the daughter explains.

"They're young," her mom adds.

"Yeah, I thought this trail was a whole lot longer," the daughter continues. "Turns out, without the little ones, it goes a lot quicker. Not as many candy incentives needed along the way!"

With a shared chuckle and waves, they head back. Deb and I rest for a while, share a snack and take photos in sharply angled morning light. The result, a series of snapshots with piercing gold rays in diagonals, what I'd expect to see stretched onto canvas and framed. ❀

KILOWATTS AND GEMSTONES

Green heads and hooked jaws,
surrounded in autumn golds.

An evening hike seems in order, so we drive a short distance from Campbell River to Elk Falls Provincial Park. While the Beaver Lodge Lands have a history of forestry, Elk Falls is associated with hydroelectricity by way of BC Hydro. Despite the impact of heavy industry, a sizable area is protected, welcoming to hikers, secluded yet well maintained. The falls themselves, an impressive 25 metre chute of rumbling white water, are visible from an accessible trail, boardwalk and viewing platform. Along with the Campbell River, the Quinsam River flows through the park, where salmon spawn and trout fishing is another draw for campers and day trippers.

I remember standing on rivers like these, casting for trout with Dad. Brook trout were especially fun, their rainbow spots like velvet pads of precious gems. The falls themselves, however, remind me of salmon runs. One in particular. An unsanctioned field trip, a school day, when Dad busted me out of fourth grade to watch sockeye spawn in the Adams River near the town of Salmon Arm. We stood on eroding banks, watching the one-way parade, the fish akin to war-weary veterans, finding their way from the sea, untraceable scents and primordial homing. The water teemed, green heads with hooked jaws, scales silver and red, surrounded in autumn golds. Fish with the look of those who've lived too long, eager to finally say "when."

Here at Elk Falls the visual power of the water is what grabs, cementing you in place. Similar to the noise of the CF-18 in flight, but a sound without aggression, just untamed natural force. I suppose an engineer might look at this and calculate kilowatt hours. But I find the unending tumble of water cascading into the gorge suspends time. I let my eye trace the river, its course bulging above the falls, then a plummeting drop, colour shifting from blue-green to pearl, the froth of aeration as white water takes flight, hesitating in crystal reflections.

Now, as sun sets, the forest seems to have doubled in height, plunging us into gloomy dark as though thrust into Grimm Brothers woods. With an unspoken glance at each other, we decide venturing out on unfamiliar trail would be foolish. So we enjoy the falls a while longer then locate the car in dusk for a darkening, headlight drive to our home atop the garage. ❖

NUU-CHAH-NULTH AND KWAKWAKA'WAKW LAND

A place of candles, puzzles and paperbacks.

Most of this season we're spending on Coast Salish land, Vancouver Island's southeast. Venturing north, however, takes us into Kwakwaka'wakw territory, while the other primary tract of land along Big Island's west side is home to the Nuu-chah-nulth. These three geographic tribal regions: Coast Salish, Kwakwaka'wakw and Nuu-chah-nulth, are home to over 50 Indigenous Nations.

Last time we toured the area we stayed in the south of Big Island, exploring Sooke and Port Renfrew, next door to Carmanah Walbran Provincial Park and Pacific Rim National Park Reserve with its famous West Coast Trail. It's in the Carmanah that some of the world's largest spruce trees reside. Trees 100 metres high and eight centuries old, growth that sprouted from soil as the Magna Carta was being written.

We stayed on the land of the Coast Salish T'souke Nation, a place I'll remember as magical. Friendly people, poor cell service, power outages, candles, puzzles and paperbacks. A place of low blood pressure. When we arrived, a friend messaged me, saying I should read Bob Dylan's *Chronicles: Volume One*. And as we unpacked, I realized a crisp new paperback version of that very book was already there, on a bedside table, left by a previous guest. Perhaps with a prescient smile.

Before that, we ventured out to the west side of Big Island. We visited Tla o qui aht territory and the town of Tofino, where surfing draws people in summer, storm watching in winter. It's a busy tourist and food destination, swelling in size for brief summers. The sprawl of Long Beach plays top billing, with nothing between you and Japan but the stadium roar of the North Pacific.

I'd returned to the coast of **Yuułuʔiłʔatḥ** territory outside of Ucluelet to fish for salmon, halibut and cod. From Barkley Sound, we burbled our way past the Broken Group Islands archipelago, a hundred islets protecting the waters of Pacific Rim National Park Reserve. Sea lions and seals were blubbery companions, petrels skimmed the surface and murrelets bobbed on the chop with indifference.

If we were to carry on around the top end of Big Island, we'd find ourselves on Kwakwaka'wakw land, a place I'd come to before to tackle the sea in a kayak. I'd gotten a lift in a shuttle, a rickety van with no shocks, from Campbell River to Telegraph Cove with a guide and one other traveller, and we took to the water in search of orcas.

Telegraph Cove's an attractive, popular destination. Bright painted shops, a boardwalk and museum are constructed on stilts over water next to a rocky shore. A century ago it was simply a telegraph shack, keeping commercial fishermen and loggers connected to the rest of the world. Eventually, a sawmill was built, along with a fish-salting factory, and a small community grew around it. Now it's a bit of a scene.

With a perfunctory walk through the village, I'd jumped aboard a water taxi with my new kayaker friends and the three of us were hauled into lumpy grey sea. Outside the cove sits Alert Bay, with Sointula Island past that. Hanson Island lay dead ahead, until we veered to starboard, glimpsing Harbledown Island en route to our destination, an island called West Cracroft. Dall's porpoises leapt near our boat, a sturdy little Boston Whaler in shiny aluminum, while Pacific white-sided dolphins rolled and dove in the distance.

South of us on Big Island was Lower Tsitika River Provincial Park, but what brought us to this stretch of Johnstone Strait were the whales. It's part of the Inside Passage, a throughway for cruise ships going to and coming from Alaska. The first piece of advice from our guide for kayaking these waters: "When a cruise ship goes past, you got 20 minutes before the wake reaches us. Paddle *away* from the cliffs, or else you'll be crushed by the waves."

The three of us camped for a week in rainforest, an exercise in living while wet. And for the first time in my life I heard forest trees sing. There's a musicality in the woods, beyond the earthy energy emanating from humus and greenery. Western red cedar, Sitka spruce and sky-high Douglas fir each have a place in the choir: altos and tenors, with the occasional basso profundo. As raindrops fall, needles and cones diffuse water in tempoed rivulets. Between brook-like trickles, drops ring like Sunday bells. *Plink-plink. Plonk. Pit-pit, pit-pit.* Each with its very own pitch. Yes, there's a pitch in the resinous pitch, echoes in amber, as well.

Sometime later, I'd be visiting a luthier buddy in his workshop overlooking the Celtic Sea. British born, he trained as an apprentice in Spain, bringing his classical guitar-making expertise to the UK's West Country. Slabs of hourglass lumber hung curing in the humidor conditions of his converted barn workspace, wood in palettes of ash, red and copper.

"Western red cedar's my favourite," he said in a conspiratorial hush, like a parent admitting with guilt which child they truly love best. "It's the most musical of the woods. Here. Listen."

And he tapped some spruce, then tapped some red cedar.

Tink-tink. Then *tinngk.*

Subtle to my ear but discernible all the same. The timbre of timber. Forest music. I thought of that week in the woods, enshrouded in damp musicality, along with the teachings of the area's first residents. Mother Cedar remains a paramount tree to the forest. Resistant to rot, a fallen cedar assumes the role of nurse log, giving life for a hundred years more. And for those living in and off of the woods, cedar's invaluable. You can feed, clothe and shelter a family with it. Split it into lumber, weave it into cloth, rope and nets, nibble its nut-like seeds and brew medicinal tea from its boughs. Which is what we did for that week in the forest. Our food supply wasn't great, and much of it spoiled in the damp. But pots of cedar-bough tea became a welcome restorative that fooled us into feeling less hungry. ❖

COFFEE WITH OTTERS

A sea-carved swath of sandstone.

Filling our artisan mugs with strong coffee, we shuffle across the road and clamber down a steep, sandy embankment to the beach. This easterly patch of shoreline on Taystay'ich, or Denman Island, is a sea-carved swath of sandstone resembling fissured terrace tiles. Each flat, right-angled stone looks as though it's been laid into place by a mason, one of those wonderful feats of nature, time and perpetual sea wash.

This morning we have company. Four river otters swim and play 40 metres from shore, bobbing, diving and putting on an aquarium-quality show for the seabirds and us. And something has the ravens particularly chatty, a conversation of staccato squawks, somewhere between hiccup and burp. I wonder what they're saying, or who they're impersonating.

By the time coffee's gone, morning sun is warm but not quite as hot as it's been. A bit lower in the sky as well. An onshore breeze cools the air and it feels like our days will no longer be about seeking shade. I make my way across island to a farm stand, the general store, bookstore and bakery, what I consider a perfect shopping run. Plus a bottle of red for later. At the farm stand: fresh sweet onions with green scape attached to the bulbs, heirloom tomatoes in purple and yellow, ripe red "slicers" and cherry tomatoes in traffic light colours. I'd packed flaked sea salt, the combo of just-picked fruit and good salt enough to make me happy for the rest of the day. The bakery stop is another first (for me) as the baker takes a loaf directly from the oven, lets it sit half a minute, then I take it away to consume. It's a seedy sprouted spelt sourdough (sliced), which I buy not only because it's the freshest bread I've ever bought but also because I couldn't wait to say, "seedy sprouted spelt sourdough (sliced)."

I grin as I recall a family member (doesn't matter who, but she'd occasionally answer to "Mom") who warned against eating bread straight from the oven.

"Don't eat bread straight from the oven! It'll give you a terrible stomach-ache! When I ate a loaf right out of the oven I had a sore tummy all day!"

"You don't think it had to do with you consuming a loaf of bread in one sitting?"

The look she then gave me is what's making me smile. And, ignoring cautions from the past, I risk it, eat a heel of the still-warm loaf and survive to tell the tale. ❧

MR. SQUEAKY-BUM-BATH AND LEADFOOT THE CAT

Upstairs neighbour is up.

Back at our temporary home, the upstairs neighbour is up. Where we are now is part of a three-unit rental. And I know upstairs neighbour is up because he's drawing a bath, the sound ricocheting through our thin walled space like the tumble of Elk Falls. Now he's in the tub. Which I can tell because of the glassy Windex sound that accompanies bare skin on porcelain. Naturally, I've dubbed him Mr. Squeaky-Bum-Bath. Like the time we had a family get-together, our host at the time living in a high-rise apartment.

"Yuck," our host said. "I hate having to listen to the guy upstairs take a bath, his backside squeakin' away."

The rest of us waited. Then the look of realization and mortification on the speaker's face.

"Oh my god! The people downstairs hear *my* backside, don't they?!"

And we laughed and nodded, because of course they did.

Clunk. Clunk. Clunk. Now the owner's cat has come by, meowing with disdain. It's a small black and white job with the loudest gait I've ever heard, like an awkward teenager galumphing their way to the sofa. I can almost hear mice and small birds laughing, the feline no doubt imagining itself hunting with stealth. Leadfoot the Cat is what I've named it.

As Mr. Squeaky-Bum-Bath and Leadfoot the Cat get on with their day, I pull a folding table to the centre of our small outdoor deck, where I have a view down a curved gravel drive to the band of Salish Sea that separates Denman and Hornby Islands. A thick hedge of blackberry, holly and fern borders the driveway, and a blacktail deer and fawn amble past, their hooves scrunching on gravel. The doe carries on through the hedge, but the fawn seems to get distracted and stops midway through the hedge. Now all that's showing is its back half, protruding from the greenery. Perhaps it's found something to nibble amongst the holly, or it's playing an infantile game of hide and seek. (If I can't see you, you can't possibly see me!)

I saunter over for another feed of blackberries, and neither mama nor baby deer seems too concerned by my presence. I'm becoming picky (no pun intended) and select only the plumpest, shiniest fruit that's now warmed by the sun. And I grin, remembering a lovely bit of local lore from my viking treks around England. There, the blackberries took more effort to access from the coast paths, but when conditions are just right (very ripe fruit and a weather inversion that creates summer fog in salty coastal air) you get intensely sweet, lightly salted blackberries. Chefs consider them priceless, but whenever this rare phenomenon occurs, anyone lucky enough to happen upon them never sells them, only consumes them, occasionally (and infrequently) sharing them with someone special.

The beauty of this occurrence, the creation of these lightly salted blackberries, from a metaphoric perspective, is it can only happen when the fruit is well aged, almost to the point of fermentation. Only *then* can they be at their very best. Not unlike us, some might say.

Another term I picked up I quite like is the concept of August branches, where new growth springs from tree limbs in late summer, but only emerges from rough patches or "age spots" on the bark. It so happens it's now August. Although I haven't been checking for new shoots from old spots, I figure I ought to be on the lookout for shooting stars, as it's the time of year they're most frequent in northern hemisphere sky. We go to bed early, and despite a forecast for overnight cloud, I'm keeping an open mind. ❧

LA TROISIÈME ÉTOILE

A skate blade spray of ice.

I wake at 1:30 in the morning and the night sky is perfectly clear. Our accommodation has small, solar-powered lights on the driveway, but here by our unit, with a low fence and thick trees, light pollution is nonexistent. I lie flat on the ground, looking up, and a gap in the foliage gives me a sweeping planetarium view. Every constellation, it seems, is up there. I can make out Orion, the Big Dipper, an outline of what I think is Ursa Major (how anyone thought *that* looks like a bear is beyond me) and, as my eyes adjust, the distant, mind-boggling smear of the Milky Way.

It takes me back once more to childhood, on our dock that ran from the grass to the lake in two sections, one fixed and one floating. On warm summer nights like this we'd camp out, "sleeping wild" on the floating part of the pier. Sleeping bags on thick foam, pillows and a flashlight. We'd stay awake as long as we could, watching for shooting stars. I don't remember knowing the fact that this time of year is best for viewing; I simply felt lucky to occasionally see meteors. If rain came we'd wait, see if it was a passing squall or one of those that had come to stay, serious downpours that made us laugh and scramble to gather soggy gear and run to the house, towel down and go to bed, proper bed, and try again some other night.

Lying on the ground here on Denman it's as though I'm back on the pier, next to Dad, occasionally a sister or mom. Same stars. Same feeling. One of timelessness. And the drifting sense of meditation and utter connection. I watch and wait. A part of me is aware of the passing of time, that part that too quickly forgets how to be in nature, with nature. The part numbed by devices, elevators and sirens. Until I remember the mindset of fishing. And realize that's what I'm doing here now. Fishing for stars. And the nagging sense of time dissipates, vanishing into that soupy celestial blur.

Then it happens. A kind of electricity, the internal vibrating hum of an imminent occurrence. Not so much anticipation, as knowing. Like that nanosecond immediately preceding a fish taking the line. When you *know*, unequivocally. That's what I feel, then a meteor whizzes past, just right of centre in my line of view, passing the W of Cassiopeia. Indeed, chalk up a W for the night's first shooting star. I'm taken aback by the excitement, the childlike exuberance. The star flying past lasted less than a second, but I feel like that black lab at the Sidney pier, wanting to jump with joy. My own little August branch. A lightly salted blackberry in the sky.

Before long my cumulative and stupid human condition kicks in and of course I want to see another one. Not unlike fishing. Perhaps a bigger one, or in this case, a brighter one, its tail a little bit longer. I'm smiling. Happy with the sighting, the present-tense memory. And now I'm laughing on the inside. Laughing at myself. Yes, I've left much of the outside world behind, but clearly not that slice of ego that accompanies it.

Another shooting star races past. Two stars! Now of course I need to see a third. Like every middle-aged Canadian, I immediately think of CBC's *Hockey Night in Canada*, when we'd watch games broadcast from Montreal. At the end of the game, three outstanding players would be named, the game's three-star selection. They'd be announced in reverse order: third, second, first. "Tonight's third star, la troisième étoile..." It was most fun when it was a rigidly Anglo name. "Et maintenant, mesdames et messieurs, la troisième étoile...Steve Shutt!" Not sure why, but it seemed that for every Saturday night NHL game I watched on CBC in my childhood, Steve Shutt was always the third star.

Now, still on my back in the dark here on Denman, I've got the giggles. I've seen two shooting stars and I can't wait to see my troisième étoile. I'll name it Steve. And, sure enough, although I've lost track of time, I no longer care, and as I drift in weirdly hypnagogic excitement, Steve appears, racing across my line of sight, this time just left of centre, fleeting and bright with a tail like a skate blade spray of ice. ❂

MARKET DAY

A rush hour honking of geese.

I have company. The familiar hummingbird's come to call, enjoying a feed of honeysuckle, although plant blossoms have started to fall. It seems to take more effort for the little bird to get a good meal. The red berries, mind you, still shine like railroad lanterns. A loon calls from across the water and an eagle chirp emanates from a tree I can't see. Now two dozen geese fly by, honking as though it's rush hour. Meanwhile, the ravens are discussing something that must be important. A neighbour calls a pet, a goat bleats up the road and a rooster is letting us know it's time to get up.

It's market day, muted anticipation in morning air. With a cooler bag and backpack, we traipse along Denman's Cross Island Trail, a multi-use gravel path that parallels the main road, a hedge separating us from traffic. The trail is bordered in blackberry and we stop to eat our fill. Following a three-kilometre walk (and two blackberry stops), we reach the market, a hum of families, vendors, shoppers and the smells of produce and cooking. The market has its own dedicated space, a tidy square of tamped grass by the recycling depot just down from the fire station. Across the road are more trailheads, a few kilometres of track through bushwhacking ferns, open grassy expanses and stands of tall evergreens.

Two dogs play beneath a "No Dogs Allowed" sign, and a musician's strumming a softly amplified guitar, muttering to himself as he searches for his harmonica in E. ("Let's see...A...G...D...") The energy's relaxed, as much socializing as shopping, although customers are queued and rather focused by the produce stand. Once the rush of six determined buyers subsides, we load up a bag with lettuce, onions, basil, tomatoes and carrots, then make our way around the ring-like square of vendors: crafts, jams, soaps, baked goods. Today some duck eggs, shoulder bacon, sausages and a Thai takeaway of pad see ew and spring rolls. The pad see ew will survive the walk back. The spring rolls, however, will not.

Following our walk home, we drive to the south end of the island and explore the trails of Boyle Point Provincial Park. I'm fighting a nagging but funny recollection of comedian Greg Thomey's character from *This Hour Has 22 Minutes*, hapless politician Jerry Boyle. ("If *you* can mark an X, you're *my* kind of people!") Maybe because an election's currently underway.

Boyle Park offers clifftop views of Baynes Sound and pine-framed vistas of Chrome Island Light Station. Chunks of the park have never been logged, making it home to some of the island's biggest and oldest hemlock, cedar and fir. We find a bench and sit with a view of the lighthouse. Waves today are from the southeast, and as they break far below, the water's surface becomes a diagonal checkerboard, white diamonds on aquamarine.

"Hello." A woman breaks through the underbrush, appearing next to us atop a scrambly bit of cliff.

"Hello."

"Didn't want to startle you," she says, and we have a visit.

She's made the trip from Manitoba to visit parents on Vancouver Island, and is now taking advantage of being here to explore BC.

"I was near Nanaimo," she says, "and saw a barge coming in with two cars and a U-Haul. Can you imagine? A U-Haul on a barge! I think it was coming from Gabriola."

"Yeah, the cost of moving between islands can be extortionate. Sometimes a barge makes the most sense. You see that a lot with building, moving materials and stuff."

She nods. "All across the country now, it seems people are moving, out to the coasts, the interior, across the country, every which way."

Indeed. ❧

Denman Island, from Royston

Wild Daisies, Royston

Graham Lake, Denman Island

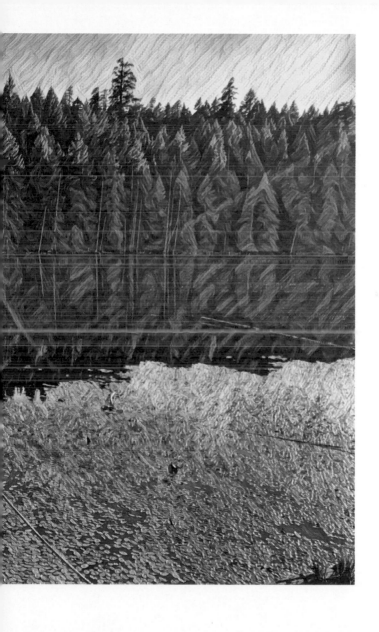

Chrome Island, from Boyle Point Provincial Park

Salish Bear Totem, Malahat Summit

THE OUTER ISLAND

---

*A feeling of being embraced, green arms
and heart of gold.*

Today we'll explore Hornby. Ja-dai-aich. The Outer Island. From our rental, we drive to Denman's eastern ferry terminal, situated just outside Boyle Point Provincial Park. The ferry is five kilometres from our unit, and as I realize the next sailing is due to leave immediately, I drive a tad quickly to get there. This is vacation after all, I don't have time to *wait*! Naturally, the boat's late. So we wait. Fun fact: most Google Maps ferry searches, I find, pinpoint the terminal toilet. Which, for a one or two sailing wait, is, in fact, the most vital piece of travel info.

Arriving on Hornby mid-morning, we make a scenic clockwise drive around most of the island. In military terms, we drive from eight o'clock to three o'clock (on the dial). In travel terms, we drive from 10:15 to 10:30. And arrive at Helliwell Provincial Park in a bafflingly dense crush of people. Mid-morning on a weekday, and this lovely park feels like a mosh pit. Aggressive energy pervades the space and I'm surprised at the unpleasantness of it. I've been away from groups for a while now, and the sensory stimuli are overwhelming. So we race-walk onto a trail, go the opposite direction to everyone else, and within moments everything feels okay as the presence of evergreens takes over, filling the space with calm.

This part of the island thrusts a peninsular jut into the strait, somewhat spoiling my clock analogy. It's actually shaped like a lopsided frying pan. But this handle of land makes for a pleasant walk, not too taxing and mostly accessible. The trail ranges from tall stands of cedar and fir to an open grass plain (now yellowed from summertime heat) to rocky, sea-carved crannies and inlets. The water here on the east side of Hornby is exquisitely clear, something from a South Seas travel brochure. But the energy experienced on our arrival pervades. Travellers here, it seems, have leapfrogged Denman's laid-back vibe and brought an intensity I can only compare with big cities. "Hellos" on the trail are infrequent. Most walkers are head down, thumbs tapping on phones. Maybe this outcrop offers better cell signals, but I don't think that's it. Once more in the trees, we resume a relaxing walk, and back in the parking lot much of the previous frenetic energy's dissipated, but despite this park and terrain being physically beautiful, we're happy to be moving on.

Then a lovely visit ensues. We're changing out of trail shoes into comfy beach footwear at our vehicle and the owner of a Land Rover parked next to us ambles up. His truck's been kitted out as a hybrid camper, with a pop-up tent roof, an exterior ladder and an improvised second sleeping platform. He catches me gawking and smiles.

"I'm admiring your set-up," I say, returning his smile.

"Yeah, got an upstairs and downstairs in there," he chuckles. "Been wanting one for years, then finally found this one. Got it from Italy. It came through Montreal, then we brought it out here." He points at some stickers on the tailgate, all in Italian. "I'd like to know the stories of these," he says. "Especially this one." And he points to a blue sticker from Zucchelli Station, Italy's base in Antarctica.

"Now *there's* a story I'd like to know," I add.

"Yeah," he chuckles, "Me too. Maybe one day." And he grins as though we now share a secret, knowing it'll remain a mystery.

We exchange a wave, hop in the car and drive away. From the peninsula, we carve our way west, still hugging the coast toward Tribune Bay Provincial Park, an inviting pocket of shoreline with a wide, near-tropical beach of white sand and tourmaline water. Small vessels are moored in the bay and, I suspect, remain here most of the summer. Nicknamed "Little Hawaii," the beach is a kilometre of soft sand dotted in sand dollars in indigo and white.

Bleached driftwood has been built into an array of lean-tos and shade-providing shelters. Children are clambering over loosely stacked logs, while nearby a sign warns against all of it – building, climbing – the activities most people seem to be doing right now.

Even on this hot, busy day the beach seems to accommodate everyone with plenty of room to spare. It's obviously a destination, and maybe that's why so many flock here, bringing the acute energy of elsewhere. I may be overly sensitive, now in our third month of island living, having slid into a slower pace. But the beach here is worth the ferry (or ferries) and drive. Meanwhile, sunbathers recline under beach umbrellas, kids gather shells and squeal in the shallows and paddleboards meander between shore and the pleasure craft moored beyond.

With shoes off, we stroll the length of the beach and back, the water warm and calm. High cliffs either side of this pristine stretch give the feeling of being embraced, green arms around a heart of gold. Our stomachs are letting us know it's time for a meal so we saunter back up the beach, but a tanker truck is currently emptying the outhouses (which I'm sure you can locate on Google Maps). So with a Gauguin vista behind us, we plug our noses and race to the vehicle as quickly as soft sand allows.

With a rejuvenating rush of fresh air through open windows, we make our way to the town centre.

Mount Geoffrey and its surrounding parkland centres the island, and we nestle up to its northeast corner for a look-around and lunch. The wait for a burger is an hour, but we've nowhere to be and settle in with exceptional local (Vancouver Island) root beer. Deb explores some shops nearby, while I eavesdrop on four youngish locals commiserating about everything.

"Tourists!"

"So stupid."

"I know, right?!"

"Don't get me started. Alright, I'll tell you."

"Look at them."

"On the bikes?"

"Yeah."

"Just stop at the sign."

"They should pull around the corner."

"I know, right?!"

"Totally."

Of course, the foursome I'm listening to work here seasonally, selling things to stupid tourists like me. And I grin, order another root beer and continue to wait for my burger. ♣

CONE CARPET

A cushion of fir cones, scrunchy and spongy.

Fillongley Provincial Park is our destination this afternoon. Roughly in the centre of Denman Island, it offers up ten pristine campsites with access to sandy beach and sea. The land was "bequeathed" to the province by homestead landlord George Bead nell, and we access the park along Beadnell Road. A flat grassy field, once a lawn bowling green, now serves as a meeting place in the park. Three trails converge here and make for a series of easy short loops, culminating in a small car park, site of the previous owner's homestead.

We follow a thick mat of Douglas fir cones, a blend of scrunchy and spongy underfoot. They're soft enough to walk on and I can't recall ever traipsing atop so many at once. In my childhood yard cones were from the old ponderosas, gnarly and tough, each one the size of a hard and prickly hand grenade.

Crossing the carpet of cones, our walk parallels a creek, no doubt providing water and power to the homestead in its day. But now, well into drought, it's a few measly puddles and a healthy patch of bog, which mosquitoes have made their new home. Feeling proboscis jabs up the back of our legs, we carry on a bit quicker, back to the beach where a breeze keeps the biting at bay. A short stroll then into the car, where I make a note to add calamine lotion to the shopping list. ❧

HUMMINGBIRD WHIRR

---

*I think of secrets we shared, and suspect
this bird knows them now too.*

A vibrant sunrise starts the day, apricot and peach, with a blush of strawberry sea. Breakfast today is foraged blackberries stirred into oatmeal with a dollop of jam, a plum blend from our current landlord who lives next door. I top the meal with a generous scoop of brown sugar, its brand name, Wholesome. (Well, if it's *Wholesome*...) I add two more spoonfuls and immediately feel I could keep up with the hummingbird, levitating through blooms on a diet of sucrose.

As if on cue my little friend arrives, working its way through the last of the honeysuckle. Only now it's hovering, directly in front of me, cocking its head. First one way, then the other. It looks me in the eye, a silent connection, familiarity I've felt more than once on Big Island, each encounter seemingly intimate. And I recall secrets Dad and I shared, suspecting this bird knows them now too.

Hummingbirds were part of my childhood, along with songbirds Dad attracted with small houses he built in the trees. Later he'd add a bird bath, a gift Deb picked out, which he placed in a position of prominence by the base of his favourite blue spruce. He'd planted it as a sapling and it grew into an intensely colourful tree, tones shifting from emerald to cerulean as sun arced overhead. When snow fell it resembled a Christmas tree, handsome and tall, and always got extra strands of outdoor lights it seemed to wear with pride.

Birdhouses were a passion of Dad's. Well, the birds, actually. Houses simply brought them into the yard and kept them happy. No doubt Dad's exuberant wonder and gratitude helped. There were sparrows, towhees and robins of course, and a great many hummingbirds too, but we also got orioles and tanagers, wrens, nuthatches and blackbirds. Being on a lake brought waterfowl as well: mallards, geese and loons. And I remember mourning doves, their melancholy arias on quiet Sunday mornings like chapel choir soloists.

The birdhouses accumulated, progressing from single-family structures to condo-style buildings that housed up to nine families of birds. Each had different-sized openings, attracting specific species, and all were painted green to match our home. (It was the only colour we ever had.) Dad turned the remote rural plot into its own little paradise: fruit trees, nut trees, flowering plants and stately evergreens. The two towering ponderosas anchored the yard. In the summer we'd have cherries, peaches, plums and apricots. In the fall, walnuts and hazelnuts. Over time, cottonwoods morphed into hedge and most of the fruit trees would go, replaced with Oregon grape, juniper and eventually a new owner.

But it was a gnarly and aggressive hawthorn tree that assumed a feature role. I think of it now as my failed attempt to become a lumberjack. I was six at the time, and had my work life mapped out. Career option one. Viking. And if that didn't pan out I could always become a race-car driver. However, that final preschool summer required that I be a lumberjack, or at least a lumberjack's assistant.

A chunk of the yard at the time belonged to the nasty old hawthorn. It was taking up space, killing Dad's lawn, and its berries weren't even tasty. Dad decided it had to go. He had plans for that corner of yard, and the stupid hawthorn had anthropomorphized into something akin to a villain. Which in Dad's books meant one whose politics skewed the wrong way. But the hawthorn, having staked its claim, decided to put up a fight. So Dad brought out the heavy artillery: a two-metre, 1940s double-handled lumberjack saw. How or where he found the thing I never did know. Perhaps a hand-me-down unearthed somewhere at a yard sale. Anyhow. It was as sharp as the side of your hand. But well oiled. That was something Dad took great care to do.

So, with Dad at one end of the saw and miniscule me at the other, we began our futile fight against the heavy-handed regime of the hawthorn. My end of the saw (the handle, that is) bopped me smartly in the nose on each alternate back-and-forth, all the effort of our cutting being administered by Dad, and with each chortling rip of the dull but well-oiled blade against wood it sounded a lot like laughter. Fascist hawthorn laughter.

After a miserable hour that felt like forever, I was mercifully removed from the task to resume my career plans as a Norseman. The hawthorn looked more irritated than anything, with a slight dent like a paper cut on its trunk at the height of my nose. After that I believe Dad paid someone to fell the tree. We never spoke of the hawthorn again. Even the species name was taboo in our home and no one dared utter the H-word. That corner of yard, mind you, turned into something special, grass coming back beautifully, and would eventually be home to a glorious poplar tree. ❧

HANGING WITH JOEYS

———

Asleep in a sun-warmed swing.

I'm starting my day with a swing, strung up in a blue hammock-chair like a fish in a coarse woolen net. Sun's peering this direction, easing over Hornby. Morning light's a watercolour, honey and amber, while the strait is perfectly calm, the sea a gold-backed mirror. I wonder what's behind the reflection, who's fairest in the land? Who indeed. With an election underway, I think of how our regional politics tend toward extremes, left and right, very little in between. Which I've seen in campaign signs across the islands. Left or right. Not too much in the middle. Drifting meditatively – my own left and right in this comfy mesh bag – I'm reminded of the time Deb and I glamped on a nature reserve in Australia, two nights in a safari tent.

"Keep the tent zipped, and close that door to your kitchenette. The goannas get in and they'll go through your fridge," our host cautioned.

Outside, one shuffled by, nearly giving a nod of confirmation. Goannas are monitor lizards, same family as Komodo dragons. The one ambling past our tent was two metres long. They've been known to eat sheep, which they prefer to eat whole. I imagined this one rifling through our fridge at night, fixing itself a plate.

"So keep the tent zipped. Got it," I said, sounding more confident than I felt.

This particular reserve, set on an estuary, was home to a resident mob of kangaroos. There was an occasional *thump, thump-thump* as one hopped by our tent. We were sitting outside on a little patio under a tarp, when Deb got my attention and pointed to a dry patch of scrub directly behind us. Two tall kangaroos were having a fight, a young boomer challenging the mob's dominant male. It was almost like *Looney Tunes*, a real boxing match. Fists up, shuffling, bobbing and weaving, then a flurry of traded punches. I wanted to give play-by-play like Howard Cosell. Then it was over, the young challenger hopped away and the champ retained his title.

So where does the hanging chair come into play? Well, a farm situated on the reserve served as a kind of care facility, the family living there acting as custodians. Every so often (although too frequently) mother doe kangaroos are struck and killed on nearby roads. But joeys tend to survive being hit by cars, as the doe's insulated pouch acts like a reinforced car seat for infants. Subsequently, the family at the farm nursed and raised orphaned joeys. Once grown, the joeys simply hop away to join the mob.

The farm family's two young daughters had a constant rotation of joeys to raise, the baby kangaroos behaving like well-mannered pets. After a feeding, when it was time for the young roos to sleep, the girls simply tucked the joeys into cloth shopping bags and hung them from doorknobs, like groceries. As they showed us around their kitchen-cum-nursery, every so often a long-eared kangaroo head would pop up from a shopping bag for a look-see, then curl back down for a nap. And that, *that's* how I feel in this hammock-chair, like a well-cared-for joey, drowsing in a warm sunny kitchen.

I still, however, feel compelled to give a good tug on the line holding the chair in place, just to be sure, as I won't forget the time my brother Norm was seated in a wicker basket chair suspended from the poplar tree that supplanted the miserable haw-thorn. That particular chair was hard and, as I recall, quite uncomfortable. But when it swung in the right direction it *did* offer a lovely, elevated view of the lake from the top of a long, steep slope. The chair was almost spherical, a large pill-shape design, and once you managed to get yourself into it you were pretty much committed to stay, until some consider-ate passerby might be willing to help extract you.

It turns out, we later realized, that Dad hadn't put an excess of time into determining safety parameters, weight limitations and so on. Norm, it should be noted, is not a heavy guy. Dad, mind you, was a very light man, not unlike a hummingbird, and probably thought *all* adult men weigh about 130 pounds. Plus, the poplar had grown nicely and appeared to be quite strong.

So, as an al fresco dinner concluded, Norm treated himself to a swing in the round wicker chair with a view of the lake from the top of the long, steep slope. Swing. Swing. Swing. *Crack!* was the sound as the branch snapped from the tree, the chair rolling away down the hill with Norm tumbling inside like a spin-load of laundry bound for a rinse cycle in the lake. As the blur of wicker and human limbs splashed into the shallows and our laughter subsided, it occurred to us we should probably check to see if he was okay. And apart from a flushed face in a lovely sunset shade of crimson, my dear brother was completely intact and uninjured. ❧

HAPPY BIRTHDAY

————

Fresh fruit, tall trees and birdsong.

Today is Dad's birthday. He'd have been in his nineties, although I no longer do the math, just think of him more on this day. He'd have liked it here – fresh fruit, tall trees and birdsong   but he remained more a lake person than someone who'd live by the sea. Two weeks at a stretch seemed plenty. Which was what we did a few times as a family in Waikiki, where we'd spend ten hours a day in the ocean, surfing and splashing in waves. Occasionally, a catamaran ride, and once in an outrigger canoe, half a dozen tourists paddling as a barrel-chested Hawaiian steered from the stern. Of course, the *Hawaii Five-O* theme played in my head as we dug paddles into the rollers, catching crests of blue for the reward of a glide into shore, then a sharp pivoting turn and we were back to work, carving the surface once more.

It turned out Dad was an excellent surfer. How a city kid from Winnipeg manages to master the ubiquitous Beach Boys ocean pastime remains a mystery. During those brief stints on Oahu, we spent hours riding breakers over Honolulu reef, followed by the slog of paddling back toward the horizon to do it all over again. And again. It was easy to spot Dad on the water. He was the one with a thick facemask of sun-screen in white and a bucket hat tied under his chin. A ghostly, waterborne force having a great deal of fun. And, like workers on lunch break, at midday we'd drop ourselves into hot golden sand and munch burgers from a beachside grill. Which we washed down with two milkshakes each. ❖

WHAT HAPPENS
WHEN YOU LICK
A BANANA SLUG?

Dipping toes in chilled custard.

Awake at two in the morning, I pop outside to check for meteors. Everything's black, save for the soft nightlight of galaxies. I find myself cautiously tiptoeing in the dark, each step tentative, never sure when I might step on something sharp or stub a toe. Good thing, too, as I lower a foot onto something that feels like cold pudding, the feeling of dipping toes into a serving of custard. Custard straight from the fridge.

I believe I emit a low *ewww*, although it may've been more of a shriek. I hobble-limp in to turn on a light and return to see what I've stepped on, fearing Leadfoot the Cat's left something to make a point. But it's just a plump beige banana slug, now with my toeprints on its back. It looks unfazed but takes off at an admirable pace, and within a few hours is gone.

I want to make sure I've identified it correctly, so I Google "banana slug." Along with photos of other examples of what I've just stepped on are a list of the most common questions associated with these critters: *Are banana slugs dangerous? Can you touch banana slugs? What happens when you lick a banana slug?* Which I love. Not *if* you lick one, but *when* you do. As though you've already done it and simply want to know if you need to go to Emergency or add Pink Floyd to the playlist, like when you lick toads. But, no, the banana slug is not only *not* harmful, but apparently their slime acts as an anesthetic. So if I *had* stubbed my toe on the little guy, I'd likely be all right either way. More importantly, my new slow-moving friend was unharmed.

Growing up, stepping on stuff in the yard was part of our experience. We learned early on to watch where we stepped. There was always a dog (Tippy the Biter, Tammy the Playful and finally Woody, an affable basset-cross who'd warn us of approaching storms with a yowl). These were not the days of picking up canine calling cards in baggies. On lawn mowing day they were gathered and dumped on the compost heap. Snakes, however, required a different level of caution. Occasionally, we'd have a long, thick bull snake pass through, no doubt looking for vermin that lived by the compost. But it was the rattlesnakes we were seriously watching for. When I was preschool age we got one or two in the yard each year, in the hottest months, when they slithered down from the hills to the cool of the lake. As I grew up their numbers dropped, from annual sightings to alternate years, then one every four years, until we simply stopped seeing them. Perhaps a window onto the globe's changing environment.

During those childhood summers, watering was an important household chore. Sprinklers ensured fruit and nut trees were happy and kept the grass as something resembling lawn. Dad would be the one to move sprinklers around the yard and turn them off in the evening. Depending on the heat, it would often be late at night. So it was Dad who had the best stories of stepping on things in the dark on wet grass. We rarely wore shoes in the yard. And one of his recollective favourites was the time he stepped on what felt like an overripe cantaloupe. A cantaloupe with warts. Which let out a deep throaty croak. It was a toad the size of a bowling ball. But before Dad had a chance to give it a cursory lick, it leapt away, leaving him to come wake me and share his new story. And I like to believe Dad was smiling just now, as I stepped on the slimy blond slug. ❧

MORNING BEACH
AT MORNING

Grey hues of muted sky.

It's early and I'm bleary-eyed as we drive northeast on Denman. Although we're staying on the island's east side, we have to drive a bit north, then west, then north and back east again to get to our destination. (There aren't many roads to choose from.) Which delivers us to Morning Beach Park. It's a good place to watch sunrise, we've read. But morning skyline today's just a bright gauzy pall. The beach, which is lovely, has a greyish hue under muted light. Away to the south and east is Hornby, while around the corner to the west is Baynes Sound, separating Denman from Vancouver Island.

A short stroll through salal and pine brings us to the top of a cliff, part of the Komas Bluffs, the beach 30 metres below. In the past, locals clambered down using a fixed rope, quite the opposite of accessible. It was known as the "rope trail." But about a decade ago a sturdy wooden stairway was put into place, which is what we're descending this morning.

A chunk of stairs has been rebuilt due to high tides and storms, with the bottom few steps now made of rocks bound with gabion wire to withstand intense winter waves.

Down at the beach we're rewarded with views past Hornby to the mainland Coast Mountains, while away to the north Denman curls into a tapering spit. Beyond that is Jáji7em and Kw'ulh Marine Provincial Park, also known as Tree Island Park, accessible at low tide with a three-kilometre walk over seabed and rock. The local advice: "Don't cross without knowing the tides." Across the strait, Big Island's Goose Spit Park points this way, toward Denman spit, the two fingers of land seemingly wanting to touch, connect or remember a time they once did, the vista reminiscent of Michelangelo's *The Creation of Adam*. ❧

EVENING SWIM

Tiptoeing on dolphins' backs.

Time for an evening dip in the sea, so we head to Denman's McFarlane Beach. The shoreline here is another unique stretch of grey-blond rock, slabs of gently convexed sandstone, the look of a pod of surfacing whales. Step from one to the next (and to the next) and you feel as though you're tiptoeing on dolphins' backs. Drifting kelp and sargasso could be swirls of mermaid hair, and the whole becomes a magical vignette.

The beach almost resembles a welcoming skateboard park, with smooth, rounded, concrete-like stone. Strands of seagrass move past on the tide, a gentle current pulling things south. Stepping with care between atolls of barnacles, I'm able to access bathtub-deep water, cool and refreshing at day's end, now cast in shade. But a few hundred metres away, on a large flat outcrop, sun still shines and a group of swimmers stands in a tight little clump, enjoying the day's last rays. ❧

OLD GROWTH

Towering firs, black-striped with char.

Back to **Boyle Point** ("If *you* can mark an X..."), which today we'll access by weaving our vehicle through cars lined up for the ferry. The protocol is to put hazard lights on, which lets ferry staff know you're just passing through. Two workers in orange safety vests *prrsht* back and forth on walkie-talkies and wave us on. The line of cars waiting to go to Hornby is long, likely a two-sailing wait. Drivers and passengers stand around, chatting. Kids are playing while dogs sniff about. The energy today is positive, relaxed. An end of season vibe.

It's late afternoon and diminishing sun is changing the shape and the feel of the forest. A leisurely loop through the trees takes us past massive old firs scarred in fire tattoos, thick crevassed bark striped with char. We tramp for an hour, ground undulating inland and cresting back to the coast, with peekaboo views of Big Island through nurse logs and greenery. Smoke from elsewhere has puffed its way here, menacing in its advancing indifference.

These woods (which have never been logged) decorate the terrain in the most unusual shapes I've seen. One stand of cedar has grown together, its base now the size of a truck. Other massive deadfalls have wedged themselves together in curvilinear bends that boggle the mind, monstrous trees threaded amongst still-rooted trunks, like the world's grandest game of pickup sticks, some unseen player patiently waiting for their colossal opponent to finally take their turn. ♣

FURWTHER EXODUS

More travellers in exodus.

Today, some light exploration plus chores. A trip to Big Island for sundries we can't get elsewhere, with a bit of sightseeing in Union Bay and Royston, en route to Courtenay. At the Denman ferry terminal a man's redirecting traffic. Just a guy shooing cars to one side. Then we realize why. A juvenile bald eagle's on the edge of the road. We can't tell if it's injured or focused on something it's eating. The shooing guy is concerned, as are the rest of us. But then the big bird takes flight, nearly on top of us, flapping up into the trees.

"Sweet," says the impromptu naturalist traffic cop, and we all exchange nods of relief.

Now parked in line, we're waiting for the Baynes Sound Connector, the world's longest cable ferry, to haul us from Denman to Buckley Bay. There's a pleasant hum of global conversation. Mandarin. French. English in various accents. And an intense heady scent of coconut sunscreen.

I join a queue to use the washroom and a woman starts up conversation, smiling somewhat sheepishly.

"Flush toilets feel like a luxury," she says with a grin.

I laugh. "I understand. You've been camping?"

"Yeah, on Hornby. Tribune Bay."

"It's lovely there, isn't it?"

"Gorgeous! We stayed five nights. Got out on the paddleboards. Just perfect."

"Where are you visiting from?" I ask.

"Oh, we just moved here. From Ontario, two months ago. To Comox."

"Was it work that brought you?"

"No, my folks are over in Courtenay. And we love it here."

Which I understand perfectly well. More travellers in exodus. ❧

CELESTIAL SNAILS

Atop a micro-universe,
same as a star-filled sky.

Returning to our current island hideaway, we drive up and onto the ferry from Buckley Bay. No waiting. Which feels like good luck, or VIP treatment. Arriving back on Denman, we veer south to explore the west side of the island, driving as far as public road will allow. Beach access proffers misty views of Big Island south to Fanny Bay, Qualicum and beyond. The beach here, on the southwest of Denman, is another expanse of sandy rock but less uniform than the eastern side, broken bits of rock in lieu of the shelf-like slabs across the way. Ancient stone weirs are visible, lava-like rocks placed in long rows, a prehistoric fish farm. Clumps of sea asparagus blanket the shore, accessible now at low tide, and I marvel at the amount.

"This is a fortune's worth!" I say out loud.

To which Deb grins and nods.

"You know what this would go for in a restaurant?!"

Another grin and nod from Deb.

At a store in Victoria we'd seen modest-sized jars of this stuff for $40 apiece. I drop to a knee and munch for a while, the taste crispy, salty and green.

Sandstone slabs all around are adorned in shells, oyster and clam, with shingle and scree in myriad colours. Other circular rocks have been naturally split into geodes, layered like hard candy whorls. Eroded fissures have formed into sharp tiny peaks, some folding back on themselves in concretion origami. I could fill a geology text with the contents of this stone-age smorgasbord, the beach a miniscule moonscape of tiny crevasses, grykes and groynes. Maybe I could take another run at that first-year rock exam!

I squint against the strait's sun-glazed surface, scanning for feathery plumes of whale breath, slick-headed seals, or otters at play. Nothing so grand today. Until I realize, of course, the show's at our feet. Countless crustaceans, shellfish and miniature snails, delicate spirals in sea-soaked tones of grey, all on a lunar expanse of prehistoric vulcanized stone. Each step a micro-universe, an earthly cosmos no different than the star-filled sky that I watched through the night, flat on my back on the ground. And while these little landscapes may lack grandiose plummeting tails of light, in their way they're just as celestial. ❧

TRANSITION AND TEN THOUSAND HORSES

You hear it in the language of ravens,
the sound of sea-wash on shore.

It feels I've awoken early today. But no, it's just the light. Sun rising later, a bit farther south, the start of a shallower arc. Transition and mixed emotions. But the outlook is good. I pack up our artisan mugs and smile. It's been a few days since the humming bird came to call. I wonder where it's at now. The last honeysuckle blossom is on the ground, and a whirling dervish maple seed pod helicopters its way to earth. I make one final pass through the black-berries. Funnily enough the fruit that remains is starting to look like raisins, hanging a little bit lower.

I sniff the air. Scent of forest, sea and a double-clutch shift in the season. This is more than a drop in temperature, more than barometric change. It's the unmistakable transition from a halcyon season to one of sweaters and the pace of urban living. A con-tented sigh with a trace of melancholy. This island, with its surrounding archipelagos, is a remarkable place. Millennia of human history. You hear it in the language of ravens, the sound of sea-wash on shore, resonating through forest, musicality in the trees. Perhaps this time around an unprecedented stretch of sun added more glint to the gold. Maybe not. I love this place in the cold and the rain as well. But it's time to return to the mainland, for now. I know we'll be back, no doubt sooner than later. As ten thousand horses rumble to life. ❧

A NOTE ABOUT NAMES
AND THE SALISH
BEAR TOTEM

To the best of my ability I've incorporated Indigenous names (places and people) as accurately as possible. The spelling of locales, however, remains subjective. From original location names, many immigrant settlers imparted their own labels onto places or retained Indigenous names but phonetically adapted them into a format consistent with European language. The result is a form of transliteration in which spoken words are effectively reinvented, changed into a newly written format. Often pronunciation of the "new" names is only familiar to those who speak the original tongue, translators or scholars versed in regional narratives. According to the Government of Canada, "Each jurisdiction's approach is different, reflecting its particular geography, history and circumstances." With respect to place names in particular, the government adds, "This long-term work is still evolving as a means of representing the coexistence of all the cultures that have built our past and our present history."

The time we spent on the south end of Big Island, in the Cowichan Valley, placed us on the west side of Saanich Inlet, the land and home of the Malahat Nation. One particular day was one of driving, our car climbing steadily as vistas opened up with terrain plummeting to the inlet. Eventually, we reached the Malahat Summit at just over 350 metres of elevation. Midday sun and clear sky gave expansive views through the hills to the water, another unique and special place. One of the draws was the Salish Bear Totem (one of a few that share that name). This particular totem, set on high sacred ground, was carved by Cowichan Tribal Chief Stan Modeste, part of a 1966 installation called Route of the Totems.

One week after we left, the totem was set ablaze. I worked hard to curb rage, hatred for haters, knowing my anger would heal nothing. And I recalled another Salish Bear Totem, one farther up island carved with the likeness of an Elder holding a Talking Stick with a look of endless resiliency and patience. When I was part of Talking Stick festivals on Musqueam, Squamish and Tsleil-Waututh land in Vancouver, what struck me was how little talking took place. It was instead a time for listening, a time of sharing. And with that, a dissolving of time. Watching footage of the Malahat Summit Totem being taken away for repair, laid on a flatbed for transport, I felt I'd returned to the forests of Haida Gwaii, where another misguided protestor felled the sacred Golden Spruce tree. The timber, however, survived, as Elders and Chiefs took from the stump the seed of the Six String Nation, the *Voyageur* guitar, extracting love, goodwill and strength from what once had been wrath. And instilling a deep well of hope.

In the lava fields of Hawaii's Big Island, locals lay white bits of coral on the chocolate-hued ground, spelling out words of compassion: ALOHA, LOVE, HOPE. The words stand out, the distinction of light over dark. It's not merely a contrast of colour that's striking but knowing the fields of old rock came about from past violence, eruptions of earth hurling magma and stone, now cooled and grown into landscape where feelings of peace and caring prevail. Another blurring of time, shifting place and transition toward something better. ❖

ABOUT THE AUTHOR

Bill **Arnott** is the bestselling author of *Gone Vi-king: A Travel Saga* and *Gone Viking II: Beyond Boundaries*. He's been awarded for prose, poetry and songwriting, is an American Book Fest International Book Awards and Whistler Independent Book Awards finalist, winner of *The Miramichi Reader's* "The Very Best!" Book Award for non-fiction, and for his travel expeditions has been granted a fellowship at London's Royal Geographical Society. When not trekking the globe with a small pack, weatherproof journal and laughably outdated camera phone, Bill can be found on Canada's west coast, making music and friends. ❧

We would like to also take this opportunity to acknowledge the traditional territories upon which we live and work. In Calgary, Alberta, we acknowledge the Niitsítapi (Blackfoot) and the people of the Treaty 7 region in Southern Alberta, which includes the Siksika, the Piikuni, the Kainai, the Tsuut'ina, and the Stoney Nakoda First Nations, including Chiniki, Bearpaw, and Wesley First Nations. The City of Calgary is also home to Métis Nation of Alberta, Region III. In Victoria, British Columbia, we acknowledge the traditional territories of the Lkwungen (Esquimalt and Songhees), Malahat, Pacheedaht, Scia'new, T'Sou-ke, and W̱SÁNEĆ (Pauquachin, Tsartlip, Tsawout, Tseycum) peoples.